D0947477

Navigating Midlife:
Women Becoming Themselves

Robyn Vickers-Willis

ALLEN&UNWIN

First published in 2002

Allen & Unwin
83 Alexander Street
Crows Nest NSW 2065
Australia
Phone: (61 2) 8425 0100
Fax: (61 2) 9906 2218
Email: info@allenandunwin.com
Web: www.allenandunwin.com

National Library of Australia
Cataloguing-in-Publication entry:

Vickers-Willis, Robyn, 1952– .
Navigating midlife: women becoming themselves.

    Bibliography.
    Includes index.
    ISBN 1 86508 765 3.

    1. Middle aged women. 2. Middle aged women—Life skills
    guides. 3. Midlife crisis. I. Title.

305.244

Set in 10.5/16 pt Stempel Schneidler by Midland Typesetters, Maryborough, Victoria
Printed in Australia by McPherson's Printing Group

10 9 8 7 6 5 4 3 2 1

Dedicated to my mother, Patricia
And to my daughter, Patricia

Contents

Part 3   Creating your new personal world

Part 4   The journey never ends

Preface

Over the past thirteen years I have been through significant changes in how I perceive myself and in the way I choose to live my life. These changes started when I was 35 years old. Despite many years of training and practice as a psychologist, I had little knowledge of the normalcy and value of these changes, nor about how to start navigating myself through what I now believe to be the most personally significant stage in a woman's life, midlife transition. I have since come to the conclusion that most people, including health professionals, are similarly uninformed.

If you are a woman experiencing the feelings of depression, anger, bewilderment and loss that are inevitable when in midlife transition, this book is written for you. It is also useful for women experiencing other significant life changes.

Navigating Midlife: Women Becoming Themselves is a self-help book offering the information and assistance that I wish had been available to me when I started midlife transition. It provides a psychological framework to help explain why this can be a time of dramatic change in women's lives. This framework is based on sound psychological concepts that have been distilled to make them easily accessible. Through personal examples and case studies, I also demonstrate some self-empowering strategies that you can select to help you through transition—a bit like having a map where you choose the route. In understanding these strategies and applying them to your personal journey, you can navigate towards a feeling of balance, a positive centredness on self, and an increasing clarity and confidence about who you are and what you want for the second half of your life. You will then move towards achieving the two main developmental tasks of midlife transition. First, to find your authentic Self and second, to create a personal world where you can be that Self.

From my professional and personal observation, women at midlife rarely receive advice or information based on their specific psychological development needs. When they experience the turbulent feelings that are signalling the need for change, women at midlife are often categorised in a limiting way and are perhaps even given faulty advice and direction by doctors, psychologists, psychiatrists and counsellors. There is typically a focus on such areas as menopause, diet, the 'empty nest' syndrome and/or relationships in general. In contrast, *Navigating Midlife: Women Becoming Themselves* focuses on the inner, psychological journey we need to make if we are to create a second half of life that is both personally meaningful and satisfying. It is my hope that after reading this book, more health professionals will view the turbulence of midlife as a normal phase of development, and encourage women to use their energy for increased personal awareness and wise midlife choices.

It is a year since I started writing this book. It has been the most rewarding and satisfying time of my life. In retrospect, I now realise my passion for writing *Navigating Midlife* has been twofold. First, to empower women and better inform health professionals about midlife transition; and second, although I had not realised this when I started, to assist my own transition by telling my story at midlife.

Working your way through many of the strategies suggested in *Navigating Midlife* will be challenging, exciting and often painful, but I know from personal experience that the rewards are enormous. I suggest you first read the book right through and then go back to the chapters that particularly drew your attention. Re-read these chapters, incorporate some of the suggestions and exercises into your everyday life and notice the difference they make in how you feel about yourself and your world. Some of you will enjoy discussing the book in a small gathering of women, such as a book group. Many of the exercises, such as drawing a personal mandala, lend themselves perfectly to a group setting, although remember, you are your own best navigator; honour whatever feels right for you.

There are several people I particularly want to thank. Friend Rita Kryshkovski, whom I met as my first writing teacher at the Council of Adult Education a couple of years ago, has been my writing mentor. I often phoned her, especially in the early days of the book, needing to share some concern or revelation. Her patience as I 'rambled on' helped me to remain motivated and focused on my writing. Friends Miranda McLeish and Dr Manfred Krautschneider and my daughter, Patricia Hay, have read through chapters and given me much appreciated critical feedback and encouragement. William Hay, my youngest son, has patiently assisted me as I did battle with my limited computer skills. He has also been tolerant of erratic meal times as they fitted in around my writing. Tom Hay, my older son, Amy Hewitt, my niece, and friends Chantal Babin, Fiona Blanch and Heather Nankervis have shown ongoing interest and enthusiasm. My sister, Judy Vickers-Willis, has always encouraged me in my endeavours, often by acting as a 'guinea pig' or as an 'audience' on which to try out my new ideas. Early on in my writing Dr Colin Stewart, George Wilson and John Marsden gave me timely feedback which reinforced my belief that I was on the right track. Peter Hay, my ex-husband, has shown support and unconditional acceptance throughout my writing of *Navigating Midlife*. Many of the stories that clients and friends have shared with me have been 'creatively' developed to make up the case studies in this book. Names and details have been deliberately altered in the text for the sake of anonymity. Thank you to Rita Kryshkovski, John Bolton, Carol Nelson and Wendy Grace for allowing me to draw on material and experiences from their workshops.

A special thank you to the wonderful team from Allen & Unwin. Annette Barlow, the Senior Commissioning Editor, was the one to phone me to say that she wanted to publish my book. As soon as she described what she wanted my book to look like I knew 'my baby' would be in safe hands. Colette Vella, the senior editor, Karen Ward, the copy-editor, Ellie Exarchos, the cover designer, and Rosanna Vecchio, the cover illustrator, all worked with a sensitivity and professionalism that has made my introduction to the publishing world a very easy one.

And finally, thank you to all the other people in my life who have given me support along the way and helped me to believe that *Navigating Midlife* was possible.

Robyn Vickers-Willis
Melbourne, 2001

Being self-centred is not being selfish

When I explain my ideas to some women they say, 'Oh, but I couldn't be so selfish!' I used to go out of my way to do things for other people. I did this for a variety of reasons. It made me feel good. I thought it would make them like me. I thought it would be selfish to do otherwise. In certain situations it made me feel as though I belonged. It made me feel worthwhile. I had all sorts of 'shoulds', 'oughts' and 'musts' controlling my behaviour and making me feel it was my duty to always put others first.

From when I was young until my late thirties this was a fairly constant part of my life. However, once I started connecting more with my true centre I started to feel differently about all this 'doing for others'. I started to feel resentful. I felt that often I was giving and when I wanted support it wasn't coming back. I became more conscious of my giving nature and gradually, over a long period of time cut back on a lot of it. This could be seen as selfish and perhaps at times it was. However, I now believe I had to go through this stage to counteract the imbalance that I had been living with. As I started focusing more on my own needs, I focused on others less. This increasingly gave me the space to really see myself and to work out what was important to me.

Eventually I found that I started to do things for others again. And this giving was coming from a different place. Now, when I give, it is because I want to give. I do not expect anything in return. It doesn't matter if the person doesn't say thank you, although I find people nearly always do. They don't even need to notice my giving. When I give now, it comes from a place deep inside me, and in the giving I am connecting with myself. The giving is connected to my heart and there are no strings attached. I believe this is unconditional giving. To me, it feels a bit like unconditional love.

Midway this way of life

Midway this way of life we're bound upon
I woke to find myself in a dark wood
Where the right road was wholly lost and gone.

Dante

I walk down the passage and into the dining room where the well-wishers are. I am numb with despair. I am dumb with terror. Do they notice? I attempt a smile. I move through the room. I am a skin with nothing inside. I must keep going through the motions. I must not let anybody know. Can they see my emptiness? Can they feel my emptiness? Can I keep it up? How long to go?

In the days leading up to my fortieth birthday I knew there was something very strange happening to me. I had no energy. When I spoke my voice was hollow. Looking back on this time I can now see that many of the structures my life had been built around were collapsing. Having created a life based on what I had grown up believing, consciously and unconsciously, would make me happy, I could no longer find the energy to maintain it.

I had consulted several professionals in the preceding years because of a range of bewildering thoughts and emotions.

At the same time I had physical, mainly gynaecological, problems. Some of the suggestions made to me were to take hormone replacement therapy (HRT), antidepressants, or to look in to my childhood to explain my feelings. I refused HRT, tried antidepressants which helped me manage everyday life, but the concurrent counselling avoided the real issues. In my gut I sensed at the time that these well-regarded professionals were not right for me. However, I was feeling so unsure of myself, so desperate, I didn't trust my judgment.

The day after my fortieth birthday I was referred to a professional who at last listened to me. He accepted my feelings. I gradually came to realise that they were understandable given my stage in life, the type of person I was and the personal world I was in. I started to acknowledge the 'me' under that skin and to create a new personal world. I began the proper work of navigating midlife. Within two years I was divorced after being married eighteen years. This is not to suggest that navigating midlife always leads to such an outcome.

I am a mother of three children aged seventeen, nineteen and 21. I have been a practising psychologist since my mid-twenties. When I studied psychology I learnt very little about midlife and I believe most women (and men) are uninformed and unprepared, as I was, for this time of life. With all that I have experienced personally and professionally I have become fascinated by this important psychological stage.

So often, when people see the word 'midlife' they associate it with the word 'crisis'. This thought was affirmed for me recently. I developed a flyer to advertise a talk I was going to give. When the young manager at my local women's gym saw the title of my talk 'Navigating Midlife' her response was,

'I don't think our members would like to come to a talk on the midlife crisis.' I pointed out that the flyer didn't mention the word crisis. One of the points I wanted to make in my talk is that we need to stop viewing midlife this way. If we only view midlife as a crisis it will be a time we fear—fear will encourage us to resist this important stage of life rather than embrace it.

Like any developmental stage in life, midlife brings on inner conflict. This 'crisis', or conflict within us, produces an internal energy. It is the wish for resolution of this internal conflict that will help us move on to the next developmental stage. In this sense, it is important to not view such conflict as something negative, but as a positive opportunity. Imagine if we were always talking about adolescence as the adolescent crisis. It would colour our thoughts immediately about this stage.

Carl Jung, the respected Swiss psychiatrist, said our lives could be divided into two halves. The primary task in the first half of life is to develop so we adapt to our outer world and thus fit into society. We do such things as study, make a living and form relationships. The challenge for all of us in the second half of life is to adapt to our inner world. That is, to discover who we really are, and then create an environment to suit this unique Self.

While I was working through the earlier stages of my midlife transition I did not have the understanding of Jung's work on midlife that I have now. In the last few years as I have read more extensively, I have realised that my pattern of development at midlife has fitted in with much of what Jung said. I was often led by my inner voice to the many processes I recount in this book. These were not sought out consciously. Many of these processes I now realise are ones that Jung used himself.

How do we find our way through this bewildering time? Our own answers are within each of us. Our inner voice speaks to us from our unconscious through images, metaphors and symbols. If we show an accepting and friendly manner to them, they will guide us on our way. When we go 'within'—through meditation, dreams, writing, creative pursuits or just by simply being still—we do find answers that help us find our true Self. Most women at midlife do sense an inner Self. The proliferation of and interest by women in spiritual books, talks and workshops supports this belief.

Finding our true Self, however, only leads to frustration if we can't create a personal world where we can be this Self. This is the midlife task women find most difficult. We struggle with creating a personal world where we can honour our Self.

In our middle to late thirties we are typically at a stage where our lives are busy. We have multiple roles. Children, partners, career, parents, in-laws, siblings and other relatives, friends, children's schools and the community may be drawing on our energy and time. At midlife many of us look at all these responsibilities and feel overwhelmed and caged in by them. The demanding life we were so willing to put hours of time into no longer has the same attraction.

As our inner voice gets more insistent, we look out at this world and wonder, 'Where is there space for me?' Or perhaps, even when there is space we find there is something within that stops us from taking time for ourselves. Many of us have self-denying thoughts that sabotage us when we are trying to make changes. Thoughts such as 'I must not be selfish', 'I must not be demanding', 'I am only worthwhile when I am doing things for others', 'I don't deserve', can be part of us, perhaps at an unconscious level. These thoughts only discourage us from making changes and creating a life where we can be ourself.

Some of us ignore the inner prompting for change. Others notice and remain in a state of inner dis-ease as we continue in our old personal world. Yet, anything other than honouring our Self, our inner voice, will lead to a second half of life full of regrets and inner dissatisfaction. A life that is only half lived. This results in lack of vitality, depression and illness.

We all need support in creating a new personal world and from my experience this support can come from many different directions. I have learnt so much from the people in my life: while talking to old and new friends who are also on the midlife journey; my family; and the many people I have met while attending workshops, retreats and festivals. Knowledge and skills which I have acquired through reading, personal counselling, work as a professional counsellor and developing Personal Development courses while consulting to organisations, have also been invaluable to me in creating my new personal world. I draw extensively on all these resources in this book. I also use personal reflections and case studies to demonstrate and support many of the suggestions made.

Midlife has been by far the most challenging and exciting time of my life. It has been full of so many strong emotions because it has been a journey of change, and as we know, any change—even good change—involves loss. As I have left behind 'old' parts of myself, grieved for those parts that I know now will never be, rediscovered parts of myself buried long ago, and discovered hitherto unknown parts of myself, I have gone on an emotional roller-coaster ride. I have felt deep sorrow, anger, despair, boredom and joy and often at a level I have never felt before. I realise we are all so different that for some the profound questions such as 'Who am I?' and 'What do I want in my life?' may be asked and answered with less turmoil. For most of us it is not such an easy journey. This is why many choose not to take it. However, if we are willing to take the plunge the rewards are enormous.

Most books about midlife transition have focused on men's lives. Initial research and findings on psychological development at midlife were based on studies using male subjects. When women and midlife have been discussed it has been usually in relation to the 'empty nest' syndrome or menopause which are very limiting ways of looking at a woman's midlife issues. Both ignore her important psychological developmental needs and the difficulties she can face in meeting them.

These days fewer women have children, yet they still experience midlife transition. Midlife transition starts around 35 years of age and can continue until the late forties. Children often now stay on in the family home beyond their mother's middle years. And once again while focusing on the 'empty nest' syndrome, women are being looked at purely in relationship, rather than focusing on their individual psychology.

When I mention to others that I am writing a book for women at midlife, many assume it is about menopause. I point out that midlife transition starts long before most women experience menopause. I also point out that menopause is mainly about physiological change and its effects, whereas I am writing about women's individual psychological development. And difficult as menopause is for some women, seeing it as our main midlife issue ignores the importance of our psychological growth at this stage.

We all experience depression while going through midlife transition. Jung says this sense of loss is a normal psychological response as we experience symbolically the end or death of the first half of life. The feelings and thoughts experienced because of this grief have to be worked through before the second half of life can be ushered in. With the use of tranquillisers and HRT by women in their middle years, could it be that a normal psychological process is often being diverted into a medical one? Medical interventions may mask the psychological work that needs to be done.

If you are a woman at or approaching midlife, this book is written for you. It is also invaluable for anybody who wants to understand more about the psychology of women, and assist them at this stage of life, such as psychologists, doctors, psychiatrists and counsellors.

The aim of *Navigating Midlife* is to inform you about the psychological importance of the middle years, and to validate the range of thoughts and emotions you will experience around this time. It also includes information and practical, verified strategies that will empower you to find your authentic Self, and to create a new personal world. You can then make the most of the second half of your life.

Part 1
What is midlife transition?

During midlife it is natural for psychic energy to be redirected
to our inner world to do reflective, inner work.
Lethargy comes upon us for no apparent reason. Things that
once interested us no longer hold our attention.
These are inner taps on the shoulder for us to go within, to
find our Self, and to search out new meaning to our life.

2

A woman at midlife transition

We cannot live the afternoon of life according to the programme of life's morning, for what was great in the morning will be little at evening, and what in the morning was true will at evening have become a lie.

C. G. Jung

Julie, a woman in her mid-forties, sits opposite me. A mutual friend has recommended me to her. When I reassure her that whatever we discuss will remain confidential (I have changed her details here), her words come tumbling out.

Julie: I feel trapped, I feel powerless. I liked being looked after. I liked being at home with my children when they were young. And when they went to school I enjoyed studying part-time and finally getting a degree. I felt fine. But now it's different.

Robyn: What do you mean different?

Julie: I've felt down now for a long time. Especially ever since I got a full-time job when I turned 40. I hate the routine of working nine to five and the business ethics of many of the companies I have to deal with. My work doesn't have enough meaning for me.

Money is not enough to keep me going. In the past ten years I've had several bouts of depression and they're coming more often since I started work.

Robyn: Have you talked to anybody before about the depression?

Julie: Yes. When my father died suddenly a couple of years ago I felt so depressed I went and saw my doctor. He referred me to a psychiatrist, and I saw him a couple of times. He gave me some anti-depressants. Dave was really angry with me for going to counselling and then when I told him about the anti-depressants he hit the roof.

One Saturday afternoon as I lay in bed he said to me, 'Get up and stop feeling sorry for yourself.' And so I did. However now the feelings are returning. I feel awful, but I don't want to put anybody out. I don't want to let people down.

Robyn: What do you mean by letting people down?

Julie: I hate criticism and disharmony. When I was a young girl I vowed to myself to never be selfish. I don't want to be selfish and demanding. And I'm scared of the thought of making changes. And I wonder if I make changes will I be happy or more miserable. (There's a brief pause and then she speaks suddenly.) I have the most lovely life.

Robyn: What do you mean?

Julie: It looks lovely. I have a hard-working husband, two healthy grown-up children and a nice home. Who am I to kick up a fuss? I feel pathetic compared to my husband and boss. They just keep on going and whenever I seem a bit flat they just tell me to get on with life. My husband never expresses any feelings.

Robyn: How is your husband's health?

Julie: His health seems fine, however all the men in his family have died of heart attacks in their early 60s. He is so much part of my life I can't imagine life without him. I crave intimacy in my life and yet find it impossible to have it with him.

Robyn: Have you ever thought of leaving him?

Julie: No. After years of trying to change him I've decided he is enough. I can't imagine life without him. I would stay with him even if I knew it would kill me.

Robyn: What do you get from the marriage?

Julie: I love being with him. I feel safe and secure with him and loved by him.

Robyn: How does he make you feel loved?

Julie: Because of what he does for me. But I'd like to make some changes. I've never been involved with our finances. Money scares me. However, in the last few years I have realised that I am 'grown up'. I want some control. I want to plan things. I want to explore options, to see if we could downgrade our housing, get rid of the mortgage and live differently. The children have left home. It's a good time to make a move.

Robyn: Have you talked to Dave about this?

Julie: He gets annoyed when I ask to have the finances explained to me. I would love to be on my own. I need to find me.

Robyn: Do you do anything for yourself away from home and work, something just for your own pleasure?

Julie: No. I've planned to go to yoga and writing classes,

but something stops me. I feel guilty whenever I go
to do anything for myself. So I tend to stay around
home when I'm not working, yet I would like to do
things. Nobody is stopping me.

Robyn: Then what is stopping you?

Julie: If I take time for me I feel as though I am letting
others down.

THE POINT OF CHOICE

Julie is typical of a woman at the point of midlife transition in
that her world is full of contradictions and bewildering thoughts
and feelings. For several years now she has been clinging on to
her old world while aware that there is another world that is
increasingly enticing. She feels scared. She wonders—could it be
better? She says she loves her husband and would never leave
him, and in the next breath goes on to say that she would love
to be alone. In the past she has wanted to feel secure. Now she
wants to explore another way of living. She is beginning to
question the vow she made as a young girl never to be selfish.
After telling me how miserable she has been for several years,
she says she has a most lovely life. She wants intimacy in her
life, believes she can't get that from her husband, yet says she
would never leave him. She has found money scary and so
happily left this up to her husband. She now wants to understand their finances and have some control over directing her
life. When expressing her thoughts and feelings she has perceived herself as demanding. She is now realising that she has a
right to express herself. She wants to do things for herself, such
as go to yoga and writing classes; however, when she attempts
to do these she says a wall comes up. Until now she has not
wanted to think about what she wanted in life, it has been so

easy to just let others decide. She now wants to make some decisions for herself.

Julie is now at the point of choice. She can decide to stay as she is and remain in the life she has been in, or she can decide to move on, to make changes and take control. And this is the midlife crisis—the actual point of choice. As Anne Brennan and Janice Brewi point out in *Midlife: Psychological and Spiritual Perspectives*:

> The real crisis is not the turbulence, the depression, the midlife crazies, as important as these outer signs of it may be. The crisis is: Will I move on? Will I leave behind the first half of my life, which then demands a whole new myth and story for me to live out of, a whole new meaning and way of being.

At this critical stage of midlife we are asking ourselves such questions as:

What is the meaning of my life?

Do I feel fulfilled in my relationships with my partner, my children, my friends, my work and my community?

What is it that I truly want for myself?

What do I truly want for others?

What are my core values? Are they reflected in my life?

What are my talents? Am I using them? Do I know them?

Have I fulfilled my earlier dreams? Do they still have meaning for me?

Can I create a way to live that fulfils my current desires, values and talents?

How suitable is my present life structure?

How might I need to change my present lifestyle to fulfil myself?

During midlife it is natural for psychic energy to be re-directed to our inner world to do this reflective, inner work.

Lethargy comes upon us for no apparent reason. Things that once interested us no longer hold our attention. These are signs for us to go within, to search out new meaning to our life. Women experiencing this lethargy can feel stressed as they try to fulfil their roles in life. They think there is something physically wrong with them. If they consult a doctor they may be prescribed a tonic, antidepressants or perhaps even HRT. In some cases these may be of assistance. However, often the lethargy is there because the woman's body is telling her to take this time out to attend to her psychological needs of personal reflection. Not everyone will be able to make, or choose to make, these necessary changes.

When women resist midlife transition

Some women ignore the signs. They hold on to their old life in fear, and as the inner promptings get stronger they become increasingly rigid in their outlook on life. In their forties they will be caricatures of themselves at 30. They will be women struggling endlessly to fix their outer world—their faces, their bodies, their careers and their homes. Or they will be still involved in a never-ending round of activities that on questioning they admit have little meaning for them anymore. In the short term keeping busy may alleviate some of the pain, but in the long term this is to no avail. For the pain these women are trying to alleviate requires them to go within. As they refuse to do this they miss the opportunity to create a life that fosters the development of a strong inner sense of Self. Their lives become increasingly void of joy and meaning.

Some women heed the signs, give up on their old life, yet find it impossible to create a new life. They remain depressed and not engaged in the world for the rest of their lives.

Other women refuse the long, slow process of integration. Instead they have a radical conversion. They discard the identity of the first half of life and all its values, only to quickly convert their life using the opposite set of values. They repress their former life completely and produce just as unbalanced a state as existed before, but in the opposite direction. For example, a woman who has in the past been extremely repressed will radically convert to a promiscuous lifestyle.

WHEN WOMEN EMBRACE MIDLIFE TRANSITION

Some women are open to the challenge of midlife transition and embrace it from when they feel the very first inner promptings. Others resist at first but finally start making changes further into the midlife cycle. These are the women who may experience the transition as more of a crisis. Once a woman embraces midlife transition, she begins to achieve more depth, flexibility and integration. She increasingly has clarity about herself and her approach to life and an acceptance of and flexibility about differences in herself and others. She is busy creating a world that honours her inner yearnings, and is engaged in activities and commitments that foster the development of a strong inner sense of Self.

WHAT CAN JULIE DO?

When Julie first made her appointment she was coming with the aim of exploring how to find a different job. Once we had the first session together, I assessed that changing jobs was not her most immediate need—it could be addressed in the future. She agreed.

Julie enjoys writing. She used to keep a journal. Since starting work she has written very little. Before she left the first session I suggested to Julie that she find some regular time daily to do some personal writing. This will help her to continue to listen to her inner voice and gradually she will be guided towards what she needs to do. Her inner turmoil and depression are natural as she listens to her inner voice and the questions that need answering. The turmoil and depression will decrease once she starts creating a personal world to honour her Self. She will need to develop and implement skills to help her do this though.

From what Julie is saying, and from what we personally know, it is not easy to change the way we act, especially when we are consequently perceived by others as demanding. People who know us well, who love us, who are familiar with us, may be upset, bewildered and angry, especially if we are behaving in a way that is asking them to also act differently. They want us to stay as we are. We have to be willing to upset others. This is a difficult step, especially for those who have been brought up to believe that they should make others happy, particularly those they are close to. At the moment Julie has thoughts that are stopping her from moving forward. If she is to move forward she needs to start challenging these thoughts. She is aware of some of them. This is a good start.

Julie also needs to develop her skills of self-assertion. Like many girls growing up in the 1950s and 1960s she has been socially conditioned to fit in with the needs of others. She has already completed the Myers-Briggs Type Indicator (MBTI), a personality type indicator based on Jungian psychology which is explained further in Chapter 13. Her temperament as determined by the MBTI naturally predisposes her to focus on others' needs. As a result she is always adapting her responses, her behaviours, to accommodate others. If she wants to move forward and take control of her life she needs to adapt her responses to accommodate her own needs and to develop and use assertive skills. This will enable her to express what is important to her. This is going to be another big step for Julie. She will need support. Although of course at the time of midlife the force within her to move forward is strong and so the biggest support can come from within.

When we think of loss, we think of the loss, through death, of people we love. But loss is a far more encompassing theme in our life. For we lose not only through death, but also by leaving and being left, by changing and letting go and moving on. And our losses include not only our separations and departures from those we love, but our conscious and unconscious losses of romantic dreams, impossible expectations, illusions of freedom and power, illusions of safety—and the loss of our own younger self . . . These losses are a part of life—universal, unavoidable, inexorable. And these losses are necessary because we grow by losing and leaving and letting go. (Judith Viorst, *Necessary Losses*)

3

A metaphor for understanding transition

When you sail you have to adapt to the waves. You can't predict
winds or storms; it's a constant adaptation. And life is like that.
Those waves aren't problems, they are opportunities.

A woman at midlife interviewed by Gail Sheehy in *Pathfinders*

Metaphors are like myths or stories. They provide a meaningful framework and picture to help us understand our
own experiences. While working as an organisational consultant I often used the 'American Pioneer Journey' metaphor by
Nancy Barger and Linda Kirby while facilitating organisational
change programs. I used it to assist others to understand the
change process. To understand our experience of change at
midlife I have developed an Australian journey metaphor, 'The
Migrants' Journey'.

Like many other consultants to organisations, I have
also used William Bridges' model, explained in his book
Managing Transitions, to help others understand and move
through change. His model is easy to understand and it res-
onates for many people in relation to their experiences around
transition. In this chapter I will first explain his model for
managing transitions. I will then develop my journey

metaphor. As you read you might like to think about where you are on your midlife journey.

Bridges' model for managing transitions

By the time we get to midlife we have already experienced many life transitions. Some of these changes are developmental, such as moving from childhood to adolescence. Others involve changes in relationships, career or one of the many other changes we experience in the first half of life.

Midlife is a significant developmental transition in life for it is the time when we have the opportunity to create a life based around our true Self. The way we approach this significant transition will depend on a variety of factors—past experiences, inner resources, outer support, individual personality, personality development and our attitude towards change. Any unresolved grief from the past may emerge and need to be dealt with as we move through the transition. By midlife we have access to a variety of personal strategies that we have previously found useful when moving through change. It is important to draw on these inner resources.

Bridges suggests that when we move through a transition we pass through three stages. The first stage he calls 'letting go of the old'. The next stage he calls a 'neutral zone', when we have left the old way of being but as yet are not embedded in the new. The final stage is when we start sensing the new way of being. Bridges calls this stage 'new beginnings'.

As I have moved through my own midlife transition it has helped me to understand and then accept that the reason I am suddenly feeling 'shaky' is because I have once again entered a 'neutral zone' as I am in the midst of making another change to my life. It might be an external change or it might be internal.

Perhaps I suddenly realise that in a certain aspect I am not who I thought I was. For me, the internal changes, the changes in self-identity, have been the most profound.

The neutral zone is an inevitable, predictable and painful part of any transition. If you think back to changes in your life—leaving home, ending a significant relationship, getting married, having your first child—you will remember the painful feelings of the neutral zone. Feelings of bewilderment, fear and emptiness can pervade our being as the old reality is no longer there and nothing feels solid as yet. And these feelings can be there even when the change is regarded as a positive life choice. For any change, even a good one, requires us to move through these three stages and experience the feelings associated with them.

While we are undergoing transition, we experience a range of emotions. These are a normal grief response to loss and occur to varying degrees any time we experience a change. When we are moving through such a strong transition as midlife, we experience a range of strong responses such as denial, anxiety, anger, fear, lethargy, depression, powerlessness, resignation and finally acceptance.

There is great variety in how we each experience the 'neutral zone'. For some the experience may be brief; for others it is protracted and intense. For some, it happens early in the process; others experience it later. We also can move in and out of the neutral zone over an extended period of time as we gradually make adjustments in self-perception and our personal world. Change always uses up a large amount of personal energy and if we do not look after ourselves physically during this time our bodies may take the toll.

If we do decide to move through midlife transition, the amount of change necessary will in part be dependent on how much we have been in touch with our true nature in the first half of life. Girls brought up in the 1950s and 1960s were mostly brought up in a highly conformist, post-war environment. We were discouraged from speaking openly and honestly and tended to be compliant both at school and at home. We tended to mould ourselves into a package limited by what was acceptable for our gender.

'Baby boomer' girls taking on the challenge of midlife transition have often found the changes in self-perception and in their corresponding personal world to be immense. When there is such a big difference between the old and the new way of being, we can spend a long period of time moving in and out of the neutral zone. We go through a series of changes to gradually get the fit right between our emerging authentic Self and the world we want to create around this new identity.

At midlife transition there is often an initial stage of intense feeling followed by a long period of time, extending over several years, moving in and out of the neutral zone. During this time we get used to the ups and downs and eventually regard the pain and turmoil as a gift, because we know it is ushering in a new insight about our Self and our world.

A METAPHOR FOR UNDERSTANDING TRANSITION—THE MIGRANTS' JOURNEY

In Australia we are all familiar with the migrants' journey. People have come from all over the world to settle here. I was born in Australia, and except for spending a couple of years overseas in my early twenties, I have only lived elsewhere for short periods of time, while on holiday. When I was a young girl migrants were called 'New Australians'.

I grew up in a large country town, Geelong, not far from Melbourne. My family lived a postwar middle-class existence. My father was a lawyer. In many ways we led a life of simple pleasures. I had a 'good' education, although looking back now, we had a very narrow outlook on life. Most of the people around me were from an Anglo-Saxon background—we did not mix with migrants from other ethnic backgrounds or appreciate their different customs and perspectives.

At times those around me talked about migrants in a derogatory way. It always mystified me. As a young girl I sensed the magnitude of what it would be like to move your life from one side of the world to the other, especially when you did not have the language. Since I turned 40, many of my new, close friends are women and men who have migrated to Australia. I did not consciously choose them for this reason. Yet now that I have become aware of this fact, I wonder whether it is tied in with the transitional aspect of my life at the time I met them.

Midlife transition is a time of constant change. Midlife development is about change in our perception of Self and then corresponding change in our personal world to respect this new identity. For you, change at midlife might not be as significant as it has been for me. This could be for a variety of reasons. We all respond to change differently. We have different past experiences. Different personalities mean some of us enjoy change, while others fear it. Some of us have strong inner resources; some have encouraging outer support systems. Some of us are living in ways that will require more effort to make significant changes. Some of us have unresolved grief that we must deal with before we can move through such a significant transition. All these differences mean that we can each respond to a particular developmental stage in very different ways. Yet despite all these differences there is some commonality in the way we experience change. This is why we can all use the same metaphor.

As you read 'The Migrants' Journey' I would like you to imagine where you might be on your midlife journey. Are you still in 'the old country'? Are you on board the boat? If so, how are you responding to all the difficulties along the way? If you have arrived in Australia, what are you doing to acknowledge and use your inner resources for the continuation of your life journey? Once you have read this chapter you can refer to the migration map below and estimate where you are at the moment on your midlife journey.

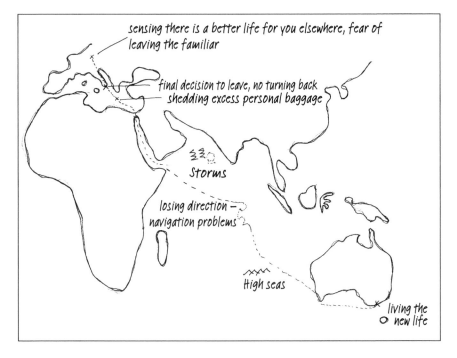

Migration map

The Migrants' Journey

My story, or metaphor, begins with several families from a town in Europe who in the 1950s decide to investigate immigration to Australia. They are considering buying tickets for an assisted passage. This means the Australian government assists them by paying for most of the voyage. They will come by boat. I want you to imagine you are a member of one of the families. Which way are you likely to respond to the different challenges along the way? As you will read in the next chapter, the internal psychological changes of midlife are thrust upon you. They are unlikely to be something you consciously choose.

There is a meeting in your village. One of the members has collected as much information as possible about Australia. There is not much to go on. There is even less about the assisted passage. Some decide to stay behind, saying they might come later. Although not happy, they are influenced by others who fear change and convince them not to go. Despite the lack of information others decide to go.

Some are drawn to Australia. They believe there will be opportunities to learn and to create a lifestyle that will bring them greater fulfilment. Others are going in desperation. In the past it has been a good life. Now it has no meaning for them. They sort out and pack what they can take. It is a time of mixed emotions. Some feel exhilaration, others deep sadness. Often individuals experience both feelings in a short space of time. As their moods vacillate, tempers get short. Many feel they haven't enough time. Others are keen to get going. In the back of their minds they hope to recreate much of the good things of their current lives in their new one. They make decisions about what to take. They pack family heirlooms, kitchen pots and pans, clothes and so on. All the things that seem necessary if they are to create on the other side of the world a new life that is familiar. They want to bring the past into their new lives. They have strong feelings as they leave. Many of these are not expressed.

They quickly farewell those who have decided to stay. Those left behind know deep down it is not a satisfying life anymore, but they are scared of change. They would rather stay where they are. There is not enough information about the new country to be sure that it will be better. They envy the excitement on some of their friends' faces as they leave. They can also see the fear. After they have said farewell to their friends, they go back into their homes and sit back feeling secure in their unfulfilling but familiar surroundings.

The others arrive at the docks. They discover they have too much baggage. Hasty decisions have to be made. They quickly prioritise and shed some of their hand luggage.

They are surprised at how cramped their quarters are. As well as sleeping there, they have to store most of their luggage around their bunks. At midday on the first day of the voyage they have a meeting and decide that more 'personal baggage' will have to be shed. There isn't enough room to store it all and still have room for relaxing in the cabin. If they do not get enough rest they will get tired.

They know that people often get ill during the journey. If they are to remain healthy they need to look after themselves. They have to re-evaluate what's important to take to their new life. Once again, priorities have to be reassessed. They have to ask themselves some tough questions:

What is most important to me?

Of what value is this in my new life?

The journey takes a long time. In the beginning listlessness comes over them and they spend much time lying on their bunks. They feel heaviness in their hearts. They feel like doing nothing. They rest as much as they can. They also know they have to deal with day-to-day practicalities and so they attend to personal hygiene, cook some food and generally look after themselves and each other. They walk on the deck when they can, to get some exercise and fresh air. Some also tell stories of the old life. They support each other as they share their sadness. Many had no idea the journey would be so difficult. Some start to wonder if the old life wasn't so bad. Perhaps they have made a mistake. Perhaps they have been too hasty.

After a while they settle into a routine. In their own individual way each is still grieving what they have left behind. Some are angry. They find it difficult to express their feelings and others steer clear of them because of their moodiness. Some have vented their feelings early on and are surprised at how for brief moments they are actually starting to look forward to their new future. Some put on a sunny face. Some are silent. Some have found creative hobbies. Some lie in their bunks meditating on their future and what it might hold.

During the journey there are many rough patches. Storms and high seas fill them with fear. At other times it appears the boat has lost its direction. During these times they are scared, even the usually brave, optimistic ones. For when the journey is long and you have no idea what it will be like where you are heading, it's hard to remain optimistic about the future. Fear spreads. They do not know what is happening. They feel out of control. They are thinking:

'It's too much for me! Will I ever feel secure again?'

'I wish I had stayed in my old life!'

'I've lost too much!'

'I know nothing about where I'm going. I can't imagine what it will be like. I think I've made a mistake!'

'I wonder if I can find out more information to help me feel more confident about where I'm heading? I'll ask around.'

Finally they arrive. There are still many unknowns. They stay in a migrant hostel for six months while they find somewhere to live. This gives them some opportunity to orientate themselves in their new life. They also need some rest after the tiring journey. They decide to live in Geelong. There is work there. There is housing they can afford.

What the 'New Australians' gradually realise is that the essentials for establishing a new life are the inner resources they had within them before they started the journey, and those they discovered and developed on their journey out to Australia. They also find strength from others who are, or who have been, on a journey similar to their own. All of these resources continue to be needed in creating their new life.

THE JOURNEY NEVER ENDS

4

The psychology of midlife transition

The experience of Self brings a feeling of standing on solid ground inside oneself, on a patch of eternity, which even physical death cannot touch

Marie-Louise von Franz, *Carl Gustav Jung: His Myth In Our Time*

I learnt very little about Jung's ideas in my six years of training to be a psychologist and counsellor. Some psychologists are wary of them. One of the reasons is because of his spiritual, as well as psychological, focus. Yet for me this is one of the most important aspects of his work. While we are living in a materialistic world and struggling to have spirituality as part of our lives, Jung's ideas can show us how to bridge the two and create meaning in our lives.

Jung's psychology appeals to women because it is a 'meaning making' psychology. From within the Jungian framework meaning is found in such things as dreams, writing, myths, music, dance and the visual arts. For Jung, the unconscious is a source of creativity in our lives. At midlife we can use his ideas to release within ourselves a creative way of living and of being that up until this time has seemed like an impossible dream.

Those who have read any of Jung's work will understand that his ideas are many and varied. As they resonate through our own life and through what we observe in others, they are also meaningful and useful. His theories link in with the belief systems of many cultures. He developed his ideas first, and then discovered these links and saw this as affirmation of his understandings.

If Jung's psychology is of no interest to you, you can skip this chapter and still benefit from the rest of the book. However, while looking for books on and about Jung in libraries and bookshops, and while discussing his ideas with others, I have become aware of the wide following he has. His psychological insights have much to offer us as we look at our own normal psychological development at midlife. If you have not read about his ideas before, I suggest you suspend judgment and read on. When first reading about his ideas, you might find them a little confusing, for they are so interrelated it is difficult to know where to start.

BASIC UNDERSTANDINGS OF JUNGIAN PSYCHOLOGY

Jung called our total psychological structure the *psyche*, the Greek word for soul. He said that each person's psyche has an in-built evolutionary urge to grow towards wholeness, particularly at midlife. To do this it encourages the individual to take an inner journey to integrate the contents of the unconscious, to bring together all the missing parts of the total individual into a complete, whole and conscious Self. The Self in Jungian psychology is the centre of our being, both conscious and unconscious. The Self is thus distinct from our ego, which is the centre of only our conscious life. It is also distinct from our social roles such as mother or business woman. This Self (with a capital S) is in contrast to the self used in everyday terminology. When I use Self in this book I am referring to that which represents our truest nature.

Energy operating in the psyche, known as *psychic energy*, moves in a direction so as to maintain balance, or to compensate, within our psyche. For example, if a woman presents an overly optimistic attitude to the outer, conscious world her psychic energy will counterbalance this attitude by presenting a compensating pessimistic attitude in her inner, unconscious world. That is why a woman who always puts on a 'happy face' when with others may find in her times of solitude that she feels sad.

Jung conceived the psyche as having three layers. At the surface is the conscious; below this is the personal unconscious; and at the base is the collective unconscious.

Our *conscious* contains the psychological aspects that we are aware of and can control and direct at will. When living consciously we are flexible, adaptable, discriminating and rational. We evaluate ourselves and others in a non-extreme way, and we view the world in shades of grey, rather than black and white. However, this is rare in our society, especially before experiencing midlife transition. For before moving towards individuation we are under the control of the unconscious much of the time, although of course we are not aware of it.

Below the conscious layer is the *personal unconscious*, also known as 'the shadow'. This layer contains all that we do not know or refuse to know about our Self—both the dark side and the light side. It holds all the traits, feelings, beliefs and potential that we refuse to claim as our own because they are incompatible with who we think we are or who we think we're meant to be. For example, if a naturally energetic, exuberant girl grew up in a household where girls were expected to be quiet and placid, she might easily repress into her personal unconscious, or shadow, this exuberant, energetic part of her Self. The personal unconscious, or shadow, contains both material that has been in consciousness and then repressed, and material that has never been conscious. For example, a woman may have the ability to be a magnificent orator. This ability will lie dormant in her personal unconscious until she accesses it. If she does not tap into her unconscious and then create an opportunity to honour this part of her Self she will never be conscious of this special talent.

The *collective unconscious*, is the largest and deepest area of the psyche. Jung said that the collective unconscious contains *archetypes*. It is because of archetypes that we are capable of making symbolic connections never acquired by learning. They are evident in dreams, fantasies, artwork, drawings and stories. He said they account for the universal tendencies in humankind. Fundamental patterns derived from archetypes recur throughout the world. Evidence for them is found in the similarity of symbolic content in myths, religions, fairy tales and poetry across all cultures. For example, the archetype of the universal creative mother, as expressed by Mother Nature, the Earth Goddess in Greek religion, the 'Grandmother' of the American Indians and the female principle, Yin, in Taoist belief.

Archetypes represent symbolically deep layers within the psyche of all human beings. It is these archetypal images that move us, that give meaning and purpose to our lives, but over which we have limited, if any control. The *Self* archetype is the prime mover in our psyche at midlife, moving us towards individuation. Other major archetypal images that are important to us in understanding psychic processes at midlife are the *animus*, the *persona* and the *shadow*. There are also archetypal objects. The major object and one of the oldest and most universally know to humankind is the *mandala*. I explain how we can use the mandala at midlife to gain greater insight into our Self in Chapter 12.

JUNG'S UNDERSTANDING OF DEVELOPMENT AT MIDLIFE

Jung called our development during the first half of life 'ego development'. He saw the *ego* as the conscious, subordinate part of our personality, the top layer of the psyche. He said that at midlife transition we are pulled by our psyche to bring into consciousness the unconscious parts of our psyche. As we do this we move towards becoming our complete Self. We move towards individuation.

Jung used the term *individuation* to denote the process by which a person becomes a psychological individual—that is, a separate indivisible unit or whole. It is only a few rare beings who have been able to do this. For many of us it is something we continue to strive for throughout life but never truly attain.

STEIN'S THREE PHASES OF MIDLIFE TRANSITION

In his book *In Midlife*, Murray Stein describes three phases that we go through as we move towards individuation—separation, liminality and reintegration. Although these three phases will be discussed in a discrete, linear way they are from my experience a more flowing and at times chaotic interwoven process. I had to go back and complete aspects of separation even though I was already well into the second phase, the phase of liminality. For example, when with 'old' friends I sometimes found I was slipping back into an 'old' persona—one I thought

I had completely discarded. I found this experience very jarring as I realised the further personal work I needed to do.

If we consider 'The Migrants' Journey' metaphor and Bridges' model described in the previous chapter we can see these three phases of the individuation process at midlife. The first phase of the midlife transition, separation, is represented metaphorically when our migrants board the ship and leave behind what is familiar. Bridges would describe this stage as 'letting go of the old'. The second stage, liminality, is represented metaphorically when the migrants are out in the middle of the ocean. Bridges called this stage 'the neutral zone'. The final stage, reintegration, is represented metaphorically when our migrants land in Australia and start the arduous work of creating a new life. Bridges aptly called this stage 'new beginnings'.

SEPARATION

At the beginning of midlife transition we start observing our persona from the first half of life to determine which parts are truly us. The persona is the mask we wear as we interact with others in our daily lives. The word persona comes from the Latin word for mask and actors wore them on the ancient stage. Depending on the situation and the people we are with, we will present different personae. For example, I might present an outgoing persona with my friends and a reserved persona with my clients. The masks, the personae, then become the conscious idea of ourselves, and in all the different forms become our ego.

At this first phase of midlife transition we have to let go of the masks we have built up over many years. This process escalated for me on my fortieth birthday. I didn't realise then what was happening to me. Up until this time the persona I presented to the people around me was that of the outgoing, able, coping, industrious mother, wife and career woman. For several years I had sensed an inner change; however, my perception of Self changed dramatically on and around that night as friends and family saw this other part of my Self. In his book *In Midlife* Stein explains:

> a 'crack' can open in the identity between the ego and this persona, between 'who I now feel I am' and 'who I have appeared to be in my own eyes and in the eyes of others in the past'.

When this happened to me on my fortieth birthday, it was terrifying. It was as though many of the ideals, hopes, beliefs, attitudes and structures I had built my life around were disappearing. As terrifying as this sudden crack in the identity is, it is often the best way, for otherwise the ego's natural defences will pull the persona back into place, even though it will now appear a little false. Therefore some people will experience the crack and be terrified at the thought of leaving their persona identification behind. They pretend nothing has happened and continue living as they have in the past although a psychological unease can be detected in increasingly rigid, outmoded and anxious behaviour.

For example, a woman might refuse to stop mothering although her children are now adults. Her life will be full of depression and vague longing, nostalgia and regret as she has not wanted to recognise and accept the changes as her children have moved towards independence. In many ways this response is understandable if her children have been the main focus of her life. She wants to deny what is happening, keep the persona of mother and not have to deal with the major losses and changes involved. As Stein explains:

Actual deep-going psychological separation from an earlier persona, and from the sense of identity that goes with it, seems to require both a conscious and an unconscious recognition of the change.

If it is only done consciously parts of the old persona get buried in the unconscious and then influence consciousness and behaviour in a variety of ways. For example, the woman previously mentioned may consciously support the marriage of her son; however, she may then unconsciously undermine his emotional separation from her to his wife.

Once separation starts we need time to let go of old structures and to put the past to rest by grieving, mourning and then moving on. This is the time when we experience depression, death anxiety and an obsessive re-evaluation of life goals as we lose our life dreams. Jung said that our focus on death at this stage is not a focus on our own death, but us experiencing the death of our first stage of life, the completion of separation.

At separation I experienced a range of intense emotions— grief and anger at what hadn't been; fear for my unknown future; and disillusionment with my present life. These emotions often led to physical and emotional exhaustion. During this time counselling, journal writing, reflective time and talking to friends were of great benefit to me as I was able to feel and express the strong emotions that had been swilling around inside me for several years.

At this stage of separation much of my energy was directed towards:

- separating my own values from those of others around me;
- developing an increased awareness of my personae, or

masks, and determining which were part of my authentic
Self and which I wanted to discard;

- grieving for my unrealised past and all the losses involved
  with a changing sense of Self. Accepting that I wasn't the
  woman I thought I was;
- finding a balance between this grieving and moving
  forwards;
- noticing my inner thoughts and discerning the impact of
  family, friends and societal messages on my present life;
- forgiving myself and others; and
- becoming aware of new possibilities for my life.

LIMINALITY

Once we have separated from many of our masks we move on
to the second phase of the individuation process, liminality.
This phase is seen as the central experience of the midlife
journey. It is the time when the ego becomes detached from its
original identification and floats. In Latin, *limen* means threshold
or doorway, a space betwixt and between. There are strong
feelings of confusion, bewilderment, disorientation, alienation,
fragmentation and drift as we let go of our old self and personal
world and float towards the not yet known more complete Self
and newly created personal world.

During this time I was running my consultancy business
and a family home with my husband and three children. I still
remember spending afternoons lying on the trampoline in our
front garden just looking at the clouds, observing myself at the
time and thinking 'How odd!' yet also having no inclination to
do anything else. Other times I would experience such anxiety
that I would ride my bike ten kilometres because the release of
endorphins would temporarily lower my anxiety. During these

times my mind was 'chewing over' many thoughts and feelings that I experienced as 'inner chatter' and turmoil. I was still functioning normally in the outside world. However, although I did not know consciously why I was doing it, I now know it was important to give myself the time to be on my own, to dream and daydream and to tap into my unconscious.

In liminality we are like the migrants on board their boat on the way to Australia. They know they have left behind their old identity and their old life. They are not sure what it is like where they are going. Many find this time terrifying. Some start doubting that they can create a new life and wonder whether they could return to the old. Others feel scared yet also excited as they wonder what lies ahead. They are hopeful that aspects of who they have been in the past will be useful in the future, but at this stage they are not sure.

During this time we often feel a pull back to the familiar. With our old structures gone we no longer feel secure. We may get caught up in old patterns and messages that we know are no longer appropriate. However, if we give ourselves the time to notice our Self and reflect on what is happening to us, we can acknowledge a momentary relapse, realise there is more work to be done, and then move on to refocus on our future. Throughout this time I found it was vital to place some routine and structure in my day. These were things that did not change, because I controlled them. They gave me some sense of security while much of my world was changing. For example, I had some rituals around the early morning—meditating, walking my golden retriever, Bertie, and eating breakfast in a leisurely way where possible.

During liminality we come closer to our unconscious. At this stage dreams, inner images, daydreams and writing helped me identify new parts of my Self and new directions for my life. I was also becoming more authentic in my relationships. Questions passing through my mind at liminality were:

- If I am not the person I thought I was, who am I?
- What is me and what isn't me?
- Am I ever going to feel 'normal' again?
- What is the right direction for me?
- What's important to me? What do I want to make time for?
- How can I create what I want?

REINTEGRATION

During the third phase, reintegration, we move in to the second half of life. We let go of old parts of ourselves that no longer fit. This can be very painful. As we do this we gradually reconise the value of our past, both its ups and downs, in contributing to our new life and Self. Similarly, as for our migrants landing in Australia and setting up a new life, this process of reintegration, or assimilation, takes time. After much hard work life starts to feel easier. We are comfortable in our skin. We are accepting of who we are. Our life becomes increasingly integrated. There is a fit between our inner Self and the person we show to the world, the companionship we keep and the lifestyle we choose.

At times we move back in to the liminality phase of psychologically floating. However, this time might only continue for a couple of days to a couple of weeks. Now when I am in liminality I remind myself to feel excited, rather than scared, as I know that I am likely to bring to consciousness another part of my Self. My reward is a more complete feeling of Self.

After reintegration we are flexible and open to continued personal growth and change. We continue to integrate unconscious material and seek out time for solitude. Inner work continues through writing, meditation, counselling, creative pursuits, dreams and dream analysis.

Reintegration involves a shift in focus from ego and persona to Self. We continue to discard old roles and become more sure of our Self. We have a sense of 'standing on solid ground'. We no longer look outside ourselves for the answers. We have an internal authority we can turn to. Some of my key tasks at reintegration have been:

- reassessing my goals;
- increasing my awareness of what was my ego and what was my Self;
- continuing to integrate opposites;
- remaining open to ongoing change and development;
- developing increased congruence in all aspects of my life; and
- enjoying living within the rhythm of my life—going with the flow.

By the time we are in the reintegration phase others will perceive us as natural, open, centred, authentic, accepting and joyous. We will be aware of an ease within ourself and an excitement about life that at times feels like magic.

Part 2
Finding your true Self

How do we find our way through this bewildering time?
Our own answers are within each of us.
Our inner voice speaks to us from our unconscious through
images, metaphors and symbols. If we show a friendly and
accepting manner to them, they will guide us on our way.
When we go within through creative pursuits, meditation,
dreams, writing, or simply being still, we do find answers that
help us find our true Self.

Noticing your Self

*When we are alone and quiet we are afraid that something will be
whispered in our ear, and so we hate the silence and drug ourselves
with social life.*

Friedrich Nietzsche

I want to start this chapter with a story that may seem un-
remarkable to you. Yet, for me it was life-changing. In my
mid-thirties years ago I was sitting in my front room. I had taken
long service leave from my part-time position as an educational
psychologist, and my three young children were at school and
family day care. I decided to light a fire and sit in my living room.
This was very unusual behaviour for me. First, to light a fire
during the day, but even more unusual was for me to sit. And
I mean just sit. Not read. Not do anything but sit. Nobody had
suggested I do it.

So there I was on a cold winter's day at home by myself sitting
in a comfortable armchair in front of the fire. Sounds wonderful,
doesn't it? It wasn't. It felt uncomfortable and unfamiliar. I felt
heavy and sad. I sat and the more I sat, the heavier I felt. My
body was aching. I kept on sitting and the more I noticed 'me'
the more I realised that all these sensations were constantly
there. Why hadn't I noticed them before? Or had I? A while

before this time I remember saying to a friend, 'When I stop, my body aches all over.' It was just a passing comment but one I do remember, although at the time I did not choose to think about it further. For the rest of the morning I vacillated between sitting still and noticing, and reading rather distractedly. And since then, a string of events have happened to confirm my belief that from that moment on I was in contact with something new and important—my inner voice, my inner guide. And now when clients come to me in crisis I encourage them to take time each day to be still. Not to run away from the uncomfortable sensations and feelings that arise, but rather to start listening to what their body and inner guide is trying to tell them.

We can listen to our Self at four levels. First, we can notice our physical self. Our physical body is like a car—when it is in trouble the warning lights come on. It seems pretty obvious when stated, yet how many of us—when we have a headache, a backache, a skin rash—see the solution as using some medication to take these signs away. Might it not be wise to also ask ourself what in our life might be causing these symptoms? Second, we can notice our psychological self. How are we feeling emotionally? Are we feeling contented? Are we feeling lonely? Are we relating well to those around us? Third, we can notice our intellectual self. Are we feeling overstimulated, bored or intellectually content? And finally, we can notice our spiritual self. And this is the Self Jung said we find when we go within. In front of the fire that day I was listening to all four. I had heard them before and taken little notice. Since then I have continued to notice, as they have been my most important guides in shaping a life that is congruent with the person I am.

There are a variety of things we can do daily to increase

awareness of our 'selves'. These days I regularly notice, or observe myself physically, emotionally, intellectually and spiritually as I move through my day. It is something I automatically do. I am aware of how my body is physically—relaxed, tense, aching; how I am emotionally—sad, contented, needy; how I am intellectually—challenged or bored; and spiritually—whether I feel connected to my inner spirit and centred in my life. It has taken me years of practice to get to this stage and I have used several strategies to develop this awareness.

One strategy was to review my day before going to sleep at night. The idea was that by looking back on what had happened during my day, both the good things and the bad, and focusing on my inner reactions and feelings, I developed a better understanding of my Self. When I first started doing this as suggested by my counsellor, I was visiting my friend, Tess, and noticed a prayer on her desk. I modified it and used it. Many friends and clients have also found it useful.

REFLECTION

This reflection is adapted from the prayer, the Examen, one of the spiritual exercises of St Ignatius. It is best used just before you go to sleep.

I gradually learnt to notice changes in my physical body, my emotions, my mind and my spirit as I moved through my day. I noticed that when I was with certain people, or doing certain activities my 'selves' were affected. It was important for me to have this awareness. It helped me to make changes in my day-to-day life so that I increasingly created a world to suit the person, the Self I was discovering inside. I had to do this consciously for several years, before it became automatic. Today, unsettling physical sensations and emotions can creep

I remember the day starting from when I woke up. I remember the people that I talked to and the things that have happened.

On the whole, was it a 'good' or a 'bad' day? Was it a normal day, or unusual in some way?

Who did I meet during the day?

Did I come across something surprising: a long-lost friend, a new friend or an awkward, old enemy?

Does something special come to mind? The sight of the morning light on the leaves of the trees while walking . . . a beautiful sunset . . . something I was told?

In all the things that have happened, how did I feel? Was I joyful or sad, angry or frightened? Maybe I felt great and was really happy? What caused my feelings and did they change during the day? If my day was disturbed or if I was uneasy, can I sense where that uneasiness was coming from? Like a sailor who is buffeted by many different winds, we are affected by many different feelings. The better we come to know these swirling breezes, the easier it will be to see the subtle movements in our lives.

Finally, I look forward to tomorrow and all it brings.

up on me and it might take me several days to piece together why I have reacted so strongly. However, there is always a powerful insight about my Self and my world gained through this understanding.

I have also pursued a variety of activities that have been used through the ages to assist in the focus on Self. I have attended groups on writing, painting, toning, chanting, yoga, singing, dance, drumming, Tai Chi and drama. However, in the beginning the activity I used most consistently to assist me in my journey of finding my Self was meditation.

MEDITATION

Soon after I first heard my inner voice, I learnt to meditate. By chance, I picked up a book called *The Relaxation Response* by Dr Herbert Benson. He explained that a high-stress lifestyle often overstimulates the 'fight or flight' response, also known as the stress response. This response is necessary when dealing with danger, but destructive when it becomes an habitual coping pattern for dealing with everyday life. Dr Benson coined the term 'the relaxation response' to describe physiological responses which have the opposite effect on the body to those of the stress response. He described in detail the physiological benefits of evoking the relaxation response in the body. Some of these are a drop in heart rate and blood pressure, a slowing down of breathing rate, and a state of restful, mental alertness, all leading to improved health and a sense of wellbeing.

My father had heart problems and mature age diabetes, and my mother had died from cancer at the age of 46, five years after the initial diagnosis. I decided I should learn to meditate as a proactive health measure.

I was sceptical. Leaving my husband and three young children behind on a Saturday afternoon, I rather guiltily drove across the city to the meditation class I had booked. I had a headache. It was costing $500 for the afternoon session and a couple of follow-up classes. I was there for a couple of hours. I was very suspicious of some rituals they carried out. The actual meditation practice seemed too simple. Driving home,

I noticed that my headache had gone. I also had a feeling of wellbeing and lightness that was a rare experience for me. I started to meditate twice daily as instructed and gradually this feeling of lightness and wellbeing permeated more of my life. A most unexpected additional benefit was that my inner voice started to become much louder.

When I suggest to clients that they start to meditate twice a day, often the response is that they can't find the time. This is of course one of the very reasons why meditation would be so beneficial to them. If a person can't find the time to sit still with themself for fifteen minutes, twice a day, they will not be creating the time to listen to their inner voice, their inner guide. They will not be making time for their Self.

When I first learnt to meditate my three children were aged four, six and eight. Because meditating made me feel so good I found ways to do it. It had been suggested to me that I meditate twice a day: on first waking, and then in the late afternoon. Early in the morning was easy. I would meditate before the children had woken, or while they quietly played. The late afternoon was more of a problem. During the week I would get home from work and after giving the children afternoon tea, I would leave them in front of the television to watch *Play School* and go and sit in the car to meditate. My children were very supportive and when answering the phone would say, 'Mummy can't come to the phone at the moment as she is meditating in the car!' I have always found the car an easy place in which to meditate when other secluded places are not available. These days I just use my garden or bedroom. Another suggestion is to mediatate at a time of the day when children are asleep or at school.

So if you are thinking you can't find the time, think again. Early in the morning and in the late afternoon seem to be the natural times to meditate. Get up fifteen minutes earlier in the morning. To make the time later in the day, consider stopping your car on the way home in a quiet street, and meditate in the car. I have often done this. You sometimes discover somebody is watching you from the other side of the street as you come out of the meditation. Probably wondering if you are dead! Or you can ask your partner to give you fifteen minutes when you first arrive home and take yourself to a quiet room. I have found that once I let others know what my wishes are so that I can meditate they have always been happy to respect them.

If you would like to learn to meditate, these days there are many places that will teach you for very little charge, and often no charge. You can also teach yourself, although I think it does help to have the support of others at first. Below are notes on how to meditate. Start putting them into practice today and observe the differences in you physically, emotionally, intellectually and spiritually.

A SIMPLE MEDITATION TECHNIQUE

Meditation allows us to temporarily close off from the outside world and produces a response in us that scientists call the relaxation response. This response counteracts all the effects built up by the stress response. Even if you don't always achieve a meditative state, sitting like this twice a day will be good for you. You can of course use this technique any time during the day when you want to feel more relaxed.

- Sit in a quiet, comfortable place.
- Close your eyes.
- Deeply relax all your muscles by breathing in, and then, as you breathe out, imagine any tension in your body flowing out with your breath.
- Breathe through your nose in a relaxed way—focus your attention on where you feel the air moving in and out of your nostrils.
- Continue for 15 minutes. You may open your eyes to check on the time, but do not use an alarm as it is unsettling. I have found that I usually spontaneously become aware after about twenty minutes.
- When you finish, sit quietly for a few minutes, at first with your eyes closed and later with them open. Do not stand up for a few minutes as it can be jarring to the senses if you get up too quickly.
- It is important to not worry about whether you are relaxing. Let it happen to you at its own pace. You will get distracting thoughts. Don't fight them. Rather, acknowledge them and then let them pass on and return your focus to your breathing.
- Practise this once or twice a day, but not within two hours after eating, as digestion will interfere with the relaxation response. If before starting to meditate your notice you have hunger pangs eat a small snack.

When I first started meditating several things happened to me. I subsequently found out that they are a natural effect of evoking the relaxation response in the body. I felt calmer and therefore related to people better. I spontaneously smiled and laughed more. During the day I often felt a sense of joy for no particular reason. I started to have thoughts and daydreams that guided me to make significant, positive changes in my life. Within a month of starting to meditate daily, I planned and went on a life-changing holiday. On my return I envisioned and started planning a new career direction. I started noticing everything around me more. I started noticing my Self more.

6

Making your values conscious

Because we don't do what we want to do,
We do what we have to do.
And pretend it is what we want to do.

Shirley Valentine

In the first half of life we are very much influenced by our environment. Human beings, more than any other species, are vulnerable for a long period of time after birth. We are dependent on others, especially our parents and other significant adults, when we are young. We adapt ourselves to fit in with these important people. We take on their values. We have to. We are too vulnerable to do otherwise.

VALUES DEVELOPMENT
Jung said it was normal development to spend our first half of life adapting to our outer environment. Unconsciously we learn to win love, acceptance and approval by being what others want us to be. Our parents, or guardians, our family, and then our school, our friends, and society in general shape our values. We learn to be good, quiet, studious, obedient, playful, submissive—whatever wins approval. Thus, in the first half of

life it is natural to take on most of the values of the people and society around us. Even at adolescence, as we break away from parents, we will move towards and be influenced by a peer group, another outside authority. We make decisions and answer questions about our life direction by mostly looking outside ourselves. Answers to such questions as what we should study, how we might earn a living, and the commitments we should make to friends, family and partners are primarily dictated by others' values.

Most women at midlife today grew up in an environment where it was made very clear what a young girl should be. There were certain attributes valued in little girls. Other attributes were not valued at all. We tended to shape our behaviour to these valued qualities. I was a naturally exuberant, questioning small girl. I now believe that when I went to a Presbyterian girls' school at the age of four, much of 'me' was not acceptable to those in charge. I can still remember walking around the playground feeling very bewildered and wondering what was wrong with me. I gradually, over the time of my schooling until I was seventeen, developed a persona of a 'pleasing, caring, serving, studious, unquestioning, not too ambitious girl'. Every now and again I would question, or be loud, or overly ambitious; however, this 'me' would quickly go back inside because of the discouragement I received from significant others. My home environment was different from school, although it still encouraged most of these qualities.

From my first day of school I was hit by a teacher. This was a pattern that continued until I left her 'care' when I was nine. School shaped my behaviour significantly in these early years. At the time, my parents did not know about the abuse. My mother never knew. I only told my father when I was in my thirties, not long before he died. I realise this type of physical and emotional abuse is minor compared to what many others have experienced. I am staggered by the number of people, both men and women of my age, who were seriously abused when young, both at home and at school. In my home there was no physical abuse. I can't imagine how stressful it must be to live in a home where there is. If we are abused, either physically or emotionally, when young, we will put large parts of our Self that are seen as unacceptable into our shadow. If we live in an environment that is highly rigid and controlling it will have the same effect. More work will need to be done at midlife, retrieving all those unconscious parts of our Self, including our accompanying inner core of personal values.

As we move into midlife transition, we gradually shift from an outer orientation to an inner orientation. We discover our own inner resources, strengths, weaknesses, potential and values. We discover who we truly are. There is a gradual re-alisation that we are not the person we thought we were. There is much more to us. We start questioning the values we have been living by. As we start finding those parts of us that we have buried, or reclaiming those parts we have projected onto others, we start to connect with parts of us that feel in some ways strangely familiar. At the same time we start connecting with our own values. It is as though up until midlife we have been using somebody else's maps and we realise these maps have often sent us in the wrong direction. Now we want to draw our own maps to guide us as to how we are to live.

For example, I grew up in a very physical, 'sporty' family. I learnt to value exercise and playing sport from an early age.

We lived next door to a park and most days from a young age I was in there with my sister or friends hanging from the monkey bars, swinging, sliding and gaining a sense of competence with my physical body. I participated in most sports including tennis, baseball, basketball, swimming, hockey, athletics and also greatly enjoyed kicking a football around with boy friends and brothers. I do value having had this experience as a girl because it allowed me to undertake physical challenges later in life that I believe assisted in my development. However, at midlife I have realised that there are other pursuits I value more. The world of writing, music and dance connect me with my Self more than sporting pursuits. I will still occasionally play sport, and I do walk with my dog most days. However, weekly I write, drum, dance, sing and listen to a variety of music. I have surrounded my Self with these because I value them enormously. To have them as a natural part of my week means that I am constantly centring on my Self in my leisure time. This gives me energy to move my life in the direction that I choose.

Jung said that our task at midlife is to find our true Self and create a personal world that honours this Self. Our own values are the bridge between the two. Our personal world should be a manifestation of our values because it is what we place around our Self. That is why as we develop a lifestyle that reflects our true Self, we increasingly surround our Self with the people and things that we value. As we do this we value our Self.

What are your values? I have always found this a thought-provoking question. If we are being true to ourselves, another person should be able to get a good idea of our values by seeing how we spend our time, how we spend our life.

VALUES CLARIFICATION EXERCISE

To help you get in contact with your values, I would like you to do a simple exercise. Imagine tomorrow is your eightieth birthday and you are having a gathering of friends and family. You have just sat down to plan a speech for the occasion and in it you want to talk about the aspects of your life that have been most important to you. Find a comfortable, distraction-free place to sit and close your eyes. Spend some time imagining yourself there and planning your speech. When you open your eyes, list on a piece of paper some of the important things that come to mind.

If you have done this exercise with an open mind you have touched values that are truly important to you. And it is these values that can light your way on your midlife journey. If you are to make the right decisions for yourself and to create a personal world that is congruent with your Self you have to know what things are important to you, and in what priority you place them.

In everyday life we continually need to be acting with awareness, so that we can make decisions congruent with our values. If we are constantly in busyness mode, we do not have time to reflect on whether we are spending our time on the things most important to us. Life is giving us choices all the time and they are not easy to make, especially if we are not conscious of our core values, and the priority in which we place them. For example, let's pretend I am just about to leave for my drumming circle. I have arranged to meet my daughter afterwards. I have not had time with her for several days. A close friend rings and says she needs to talk. Her partner has just walked out on her and she is distraught. I have five minutes before I have to leave. What do I do?

Do I decide to miss my drumming circle and let her talk?

Do I make arrangements to meet her later and cancel my daughter?

Do I speak to her for five minutes and say I'll ring her later?

Or is there another solution?

Here is another example. You are just about to leave work one summer evening. It's five o'clock and you have promised your son you will be home in time to take him to the park. Your manager asks if you would like to have a quick drink. Some of the thoughts running through your mind are:

It sounds appealing as it will help me to wind down after a busy week.

Will my son have remembered my promise?

Could we go to the park a bit later?

I'm watching my health and don't want to drink alcohol. Will I be able to be self-disciplined and just drink lemonade?

I want to keep on good terms with my boss. I have just applied for a promotion. Will my decision affect this?

What would you do?

Both these examples show that what seems like a simple question can bring up all sorts of conflicting thoughts. If on top of these we don't have a clear idea of our values and priorities, we can easily end up doing something that does not feel right and is not congruent with the person we are. I don't believe it matters if every now and again we make the wrong decision. However, if we spend our days making a series of wrong decisions—decisions not congruent with our core values—we end up creating a life that is jarring for our being. It's like walking around with the wrong sized shoes on. They might actually look OK to another person, but you know they don't fit. And this lack of fit creates stress in our life and if it continues over a long period of time it can lead to:

- a poor sense of wellbeing;
- difficulty in relating to others because we tend to be abrupt and short-tempered;
- poor concentration leading to inability to do things as easily as we know we can;
- ill health—backache, headaches, skin conditions, immune diseases, gynaecological problems;
- lack of productivity;
- lack of creativity and feeling 'stuck' in life;
- psychological problems such as depression and anxiety attacks; and
- feeling disconnected from life.

These effects can be magnified if we are faced with a significant change, such as changing jobs, place of residence or partners, and we make the wrong decision because of not consciously knowing ourselves and our values.

In my work I find that when people are questioned, they usually can clarify their personal values. However, unless they are asked to bring to consciousness these values, they will still be making decisions based on societal values. For example, Sue, a 44-year-old with three teenage children, consulted me several months ago. She had worked in a company for ten years at a senior management level. Recently, it had been taken over by an interstate company and all employees knew they either had to apply for their current jobs interstate, or apply for jobs outside the present company. Sue called me in to work with her and her team to assist them through the transition. When I first spoke to Sue her plan was to seek another job that paid at least as well as her present job, if not more, and hopefully with more responsibility. However, when I gave Sue and her team the eightieth birthday exercise Sue listed as her top two priorities: time with children, friends and partner, and even more importantly, time for herself. She still needed to earn a living, however after doing the exercise she no longer wanted to pursue work that reduced access to what was most important to her. She decided she would take a cut in pay and status if it meant she had more time to do the things that were truly important to her.

I use this example to demonstrate how easily we can create an incongruent personal world if we do not make conscious to ourselves our values, especially at a time when we are facing significant change.

REFLECTIVE EXERCISE
Think about a time in the past when you have made a decision that in retrospect was not the right one for you. What values were guiding your decision-making process at the time? Whose were they? Were they yours or someone else's?

VALUES CLARIFICATION AT MIDLIFE
As we enter the 'neutral zone' of midlife transition we connect with our 'selves' from both stages—the old self and the evolving new self. We also connect with the values from both stages. This can be a very bewildering time. As we move our focus from outwardly focused, family, work and community-minded activities, we may feel guilty, worthless and a failure. This leads to a lethargy, despondency and depression that is inviting us to go within, to begin the journey of self-discovery, and to find our own true values.

At first this despondency is seen as a negative. It is seen as destructive of the life so far lived. We feel the pain of loss of life not lived, and of having been deceived. This disenchantment, however, has a purpose. It frees us from the tyrannical control of our acquired, societal values. It launches us on a journey of finding our true Self and our own true values. I remember when my father died in my late thirties. I realised there were many people in my personal world who could not, or did not want to relate at an authentic, emotional level to me and my loss. I realised how much I valued those people who could and decided from then on to surround myself as much as possible with people who could relate to me on an authentic emotional level.

The first step in discovering our own values is to go within. In our quieter, more reflective moments, answers will come to us about what we most value. These answers might come symbolically through dreams, daydreams or writing. The second step is to observe ourselves, how we feel physically, emotionally, intellectually and spiritually as we move through our day. We gradually get a sense of what feels right deep inside us. No longer will we accept anybody else's maps to determine how we live our lives.

In our society there are two worlds. There is the materialistic world; the one which dominates our newspapers, our television and most of our organisations. There is an emphasis on material gain. It is a world we are all very aware of. Then there is another world; a world I have increasingly become part of over the last five years. As I go to drumming, yoga, singing, dance, writing classes and various alternative health or music festivals I am in a very different world. Here, there is often a sense of joy, there is little reference to a person's work or affluence, and people relate around mutual interests and human values.

While working as a consultant in corporations, I sense within many individuals a struggle to create some balance in their lives between needing to earn a living and wanting to lead a life that is congruent with their values. They sense that their personal values are becoming increasingly incongruent with the values of their 'bottom line' focused employer. This is a dilemma for many people working in the corporate sector. It is also one of the reasons so many women have left corporations. As these women move through midlife transition, they want more control of how they lead their working life. Often they set up their own businesses and work with others in a collaborative way, supporting each other and developing work practices congruent with their core values.

As women at midlife become more focused on their personal core values, they can become aware that their partner is driven by very different ones. This may cause deep conflict, and sometimes leads to separation. For it is difficult to create a values congruent life when you are sharing your life with somebody who has significantly different values.

7

Telling your story

Writing my personal story for this book was a very powerful experience for me. When I finished, it felt like I had completed the first forty years of my life. Simultaneously I experienced a deep level of emotional healing.

Shakti Gawain, *Return to the Garden*

Through the ages storytelling has been used to help humankind understand. To help understand ourselves at midlife we need to stop and listen to the stories running through our minds and then find a way of telling them. All stories have a beginning, a middle and an end. We develop a deeper understanding of our own life when we are able to link these parts of our own story. In the midst of the turbulence of midlife transition we find meaning in our past and the potential in our future as we tell our story.

We tell our stories all the time. We come home in the evening and are asked, 'How was your day?' We meet a friend for coffee and they ask, 'What's been happening in your life?' When we were children arriving home from school we were asked, 'How was school?' In answering these questions we tell our story. Sometimes when feeling stuck in our story we tell it to a counsellor. Writing stories has been a common practice through the ages. Diaries and journals are a way of reflecting and telling our story, even if it is only to ourself. Many of us are fascinated to read autobiographies as we connect aspects of another's story with our own.

Each of us has a unique story that must be told at midlife if we are to live fully and authentically in the second half of life. We are all telling a story by the way we live and the choices we make along the way. However, many of us escape any depth of awareness of the story our life is telling as we lead an unexamined life. At midlife we need to stop and listen to our stories, including those parts of it buried long ago. For in telling our story we can awaken different aspects of our Self and get in touch with all the riches of the past as well as all the sadness and misfortunes that we have lived through and overcome. In doing so we grieve for the 'never to be' aspects of our life. This grieving encourages us to use our remaining time more wisely.

I will give a personal example to show what I mean. In my early forties, while telling my story to a counsellor I started grieving for all the dancing I hadn't done. This grieving led me to explore dance. I went to courses on jive, rock 'n' roll, Latin, soul, African and so on. I discovered I wasn't too old to go out and dance. There were lots of places where I could dance. I often dance at home to my favourite music. I go out and dance with friends. I dance at festivals. I dance on barges in the middle of the Yarra River. If I hadn't told my story and grieved for my lost opportunities I would not have created these new opportunities. I would have just buried this important part of my Self and my second half of life would be significantly less rich.

The initial focus in midlife transition is on the past as we need to let go of the personae we have acted out in the first half of life. It helps to see how our story is structured. What are the chapters of our life so far? We can look closely at each chapter. We can write dialogue with people, situations, dreams and events and in a relaxed state of consciousness allow them, through writing, to answer us on paper. Such a dialogue from our inner Self can reveal more than we think we know. Since every part of our life is personalised by our connection with it, every event, task, place and dream can be personified and can speak to us as we write the dialogue. We get in touch with forgotten dreams and as we do this, we may need professional help as we also get in touch with unresolved grief and anger.

In rummaging through our past we may come across a forgotten possibility—a forgotten part of our Self. In the past we made choices from a number of options. If we return to these forks in the road we may now be able to pursue another option.

There are many different ways we can tell our story. In this chapter I am going to tell you about four unusual ways I have told my story recently. If you have not already told your story, I suggest you choose one of these ways to tell it. My guess is you will be surprised, as I was, with what you discover.

I found a most interesting way of telling my story soon after starting to write this book when I attended a weekend workshop, designed and facilitated by John Bolton, called 'Bringing Your Story to Life'. We drew, wrote journal entries and dialogue, created snapshot photographs of life-changing events, and acted out mini-plays to tell our stories. It was part of a writers' festival and although the focus was not therapy, for me the workshop assisted me to 'unbury' aspects of my own story several years of counselling had been unable to unearth.

I met John by chance a couple of weeks before the workshop and he explained to me a little about how he ran it. Knowing it was not a therapy weekend I asked him what he did when people touched sensitive spots, as they inevitably would with such a process. I found out the answer on the first evening.

TELLING YOUR STORY THROUGH A DRAWING

We were asked to spend ten minutes drawing our main home as a child. At the thought of this, no doubt any 'draw-a-phobes' are experiencing the same feelings I had at the suggestion. I tried to draw the roof-line of our large, rambling, Victorian, weatherboard home. After a couple of minutes I realised this wasn't what we were meant to be focusing on. I went for it. It was no work of art. Memories came flooding back. I remembered times spent in our large garden. Memories of a hollow bush where I would go to be alone and dream. I drew the rose bushes that I loved to smell, especially after school. It helped me to relax. I placed my family in our home. Where to put them? What were they doing? I didn't think too much. My pencil flew over the large piece of paper as more and more memories came flooding back.

We were asked in turn to talk about our drawings. Each one told a thousand stories. It was my turn. I got up to speak. I said, 'I lived in this home from the age of two to seventeen years. It was my only childhood home. I left it at seventeen, just after my mother died.' At that point of my story, I found that I had emotionally journeyed to a place I had never been before. In the years of counselling I had talked at times about my mother's illness and subsequent death, but had never been able to contact the feelings that I knew were buried very deep

My drawing of my house

inside. I did now; not for long—perhaps for a minute. Nobody said or did anything. I am so thankful for that. I collected my feelings up. I continued to show the drawing of my home.

I told them:

My mum is in the kitchen. She always seemed to be there, especially when I came home from school. Dad is hosing down the house, to look after the paintwork, a monthly ritual. Judy, my sister, and I are playing tennis against the hit-up wall in the back garden. Robert, my youngest brother, is climbing over a fence. When tiny he was always escaping. Simon, my middle brother is in the dining room playing with his imaginary friends, Jet and John. Michael, my oldest brother, is in his bedroom smoking. Nan and Pop are in their back flat. Nanny is in bed. She had a rest every afternoon. She was very ill when 48 years old and was told to rest. She did as she was told and lived till 99 and three-quarter years. Pop is in his armchair watching football on television. My cat, Cuddles, is sitting on a chair on the front verandah, and Pal, our cocker spaniel, is scratching and barking at the dining room window.

I sat down.

CREATING A COLLAGE TO TELL YOUR STORY

I got home that night feeling absolutely drained. I still had very sad feelings washing all over me. For homework we were asked to prepare a collage to represent the passing of our childhood. Up until this time in my adult life, when I thought of my childhood I could usually only remember the negative aspects. I knew this wasn't the truth. All those unresolved, sad feelings from my mother's illness and death had flowed out over my childhood. As I sat at home that night and prepared my collage I realised I was focusing on positive aspects. I spent the rest of the evening pondering what I would take. I had a piece of pink and blue ribbon intertwined to represent the caring relationship Judy and I had while sharing a bedroom, playing games and going to school together. A rose represented all those happy times playing in our large, rambling garden. A playing card and hookey ring took me back to all the fun times we had playing games at home together. A damask table napkin and muesli bar (retrieved from my handbag) reminded me of all the family meals my mother had prepared for us to sit and eat together each evening. And so on. With ease, I was looking at my childhood differently to the way I had viewed it for years.

If you want to tell your story through drawing or creating a collage, I suggest you do it with one or perhaps a couple of friends. Telling your story to yourself can be powerful; however,

I have found that it is when I have to tell my story to another that I fully get in touch with the emotions behind my story.

THE STEPPINGSTONES EXERCISE

Another storytelling process we were introduced to on this weekend was Steppingstones, a process developed by Ira Progoff. In his book *At a Journal Workshop* he explains how a Steppingstones exercise provides a rapid and effective means of gaining an overview of our life.

A Steppingstone is a particular period in life that contains a variety of subjectively related experiences. When we create a brief list of Steppingstones, these qualitative markers in our past reflect an aspect of our perspective in the present moment. This perspective will be influenced by the setting, our mood, and the particular focus of our life at that stage. If we make a list of Steppingstones at a later time, they may be quite different.

The first step of the exercise is to mark off about a dozen (give or take one or two) of the main reference points in our life from birth to the present. We record those points spontaneously as we think of them. Each list of Steppingstones is uninterpreted. We write it as it comes out.

When I did this exercise my twelve Steppingstones were:

1 Winning a scholarship (twelve years of age). Beforehand a teacher had told me it was a waste of time my sitting for it. It was announced in the local paper that I had won it. My father was pleased with me. From that time on I never doubted I was 'bright'.

2 National Fitness camp (twelve years). For the first time in my life I went away with a large group of girls and boys I did not know. I independently found out about the camp

and applied for it. I discovered that I enjoyed meeting new people, being physically challenged and volunteering for new experiences, such as abseiling.

3 Mum diagnosed with cancer (twelve years). As soon as I heard, I knew she would die from it. My sense of emotional security disappeared. I started to think about how I could create my own feelings of security.

4 Birth of my first baby (28 years). First experience of overwhelming love and responsibility for another human being. Realising the responsibility was for all my life; I could never walk away from it.

5 Holiday without family (35 years). Feeling a sense of Self for the first time in many years—not in my role as mother, wife or sister. Learning to scuba dive. Envisioning my business in a daydream. Starting to take control of my life again.

6 Course with Corporate Senior Management Group (36 years). Overcoming extreme anxiety. 'Holding my own' in a man's world. Knowing my vision was coming true.

7 Father's death (38 years). Reassessing my life and all my relationships.

8 Fortieth birthday party. Publicly appearing vulnerable and lost. Starting to accept this part of my Self and no longer hiding it from others.

9 Separating from Pete after eighteen years of marriage (41 years).

10 Changing back to my maiden name one month after separating. Waking up one morning and deciding to change my name. Starting to change it that day. Realising how much I had missed being R V-W.

11 Starting to write *Navigating Midlife* (47 years). Making writing part of my life. Finally acknowledging my writing self.

12 Being told by a publisher that he liked my writing (47 years). Finally accepting I could write.

We were then asked to choose one of the Steppingstones and write about it. I chose the last two as they were inextricably linked. This is what I wrote:

It was a time when I realised that it might be possible that I could write. Something I had spent years telling myself I couldn't do. I was finding out that perhaps I had been wrong. Over the last couple of years I had a couple of indicators at writing workshops and festivals—but now I had written something quite big and to order. I had actually done it. I thought it was no good and destroyed it in the middle of the night. Luckily I had emailed it to a friend and he emailed me back saying, 'It works.' And now I am writing lots each day and the more I write the more I realise I know and I can see it might actually be possible to have a life I had only dreamt of. I love writing. I love sitting in my bedroom in the early morning at the window writing on my laptop, classical music playing, a mug of hazelnut flavoured coffee beside me, Benji, my cat, my thoughts and me. It is so relaxing. It feels so right. And as I have written in this last week my book is actually taking shape and the more I write I can see I have something unique, or perhaps not unique—but a message that I don't believe has ever been spelt out before. I would love to be able to talk about what I know and then continue to write and develop my thoughts. I love the writing/reading world. I feel comfortable there. I do believe it is where I belong and that is why I have been led in this direction. What a surprise! It so clearly shows the power of negative thoughts collected as a child. I wonder what else might be possible?

WRITING DIALOGUE WITH PART OF YOUR STORY

We were then asked to write a dialogue with our subject. I was aware I had strong feelings about my writing, but I was surprised by what I wrote.

Me: You are so special to me—so important. I want to look after you, to nurture you, to make sure other people in my life don't come between you and me.

Writing: I am happy with that, Robyn. I like what you do. I like being 'me'. I would like you to protect our time together. We seem to have such an easy relationship. I think it will happen quite easily anyhow.

Me: I hope so. But you see, sometimes I just forget—although perhaps that is the old me—and I don't forget so much these days. I can stick up for myself. I can look after you.

Writing: If you do that we will go lots of places together. We will have fun. There will also be hard times I guess—yet mostly I can see lots of interesting, exciting times ahead together.

Me: It's worth working for, isn't it?

Writing: Sure is.

Me: I wonder how firm I need to be to make sure we stay on track together?

Writing: Not too firm. We want to enjoy life along the way also. And there are other things in your life besides me and I'll be OK. So just fit me in and trust that soon we will be earning a living together.

We were then asked by the facilitator to comment on the dialogue. I wrote:

The dialogue is very affirming. We can go places together. We are friends. It is amazing how long it has taken for us to meet up. But perhaps this makes it even more special.

I have written here about recent opportunities to tell parts of my story. In writing this book I am continually telling my story. I had not realised this would be the case when I started. It has just come out of me in the process of the writing. If you enjoy writing, you might also find it a satisfying way of telling your story. There are adult education writing classes to assist you. You can start writing your story for yourself in leisure time at home. If you like drama or painting you could use these as creative ways to tell your story. When people come to me for counselling, many, especially those in crisis at midlife, take time to tell their story. You might like to consider counselling, especially if you are having difficulty getting in contact with your story. For it doesn't matter how we tell our story at midlife. We just need to do it. How are you going to tell yours?

8

The wisdom in your dreams

*The dream is a little hidden door into the innermost and
most secret recesses of the soul . . .*

C.G. Jung

One of our major tasks at midlife is to bring up from the
unconscious repressed and other never known aspects of
our Self and integrate this knowledge into our understanding
of who we are. To do this we need to step out of the busyness of
our everyday life and stop to listen to our Self. We can do this by
making time for activities discussed elsewhere in this book such
as meditation, personal writing and creative pursuits. We can
also do this inner work by noticing our dreams and daydreams
and then finding a way to understand them.

Jung found that by understanding his own dreams he could
find solutions to his everyday problems. He found it was the
same for his patients. He said that the psyche speaks to us
through dream images and if we take the time to explore these
images we find a natural healer or guide. Therefore, if we can
find a way to discern the meaning of our dream images, we
each have a gateway to a personal wisdom we cannot possibly
find anywhere else. No book, institution or guru can possibly

give us such accurate information about our Self. For through our own dream images we are discovering our own truth, no one else's. If we can at least understand some of our dreams and daydreams, we gain more knowledge about what is right for us, and what our true nature wants us to do.

I have never seen myself as much of a night dreamer. Of course I do dream. We all do. I just don't remember dreams very often. In contrast, my daughter and a couple of my friends can spend many minutes recounting their dreams to me. I marvel at the intricacy and detail of their recollections. Yet, over the last few years I have realised that despite the paucity of my memory for my dreams, they have still been a very strong guide for me during midlife.

Up until five years ago I had done little to learn about how to access my dreams. Through my studies and reading I knew they could be used to understand myself better. I assumed it would be something I would need to dedicate a lot of time to learn. I had already benefited from insights gained through daydreams. I assumed understanding dreams would be a much more complicated process. I have now found it is not necessarily so.

My dream education started at a week's course at Byron Bay, called 'A Sound and Psychic Adventure'. On the first morning the facilitators Carol Nelson and Wendy Grace talked to us about dreams. They gave us a simple process to start remembering them.

1 Place a pad and pen beside your bed.
2 Say to yourself, 'All affirmations work for me. Let my dreaming self and waking self be one.'
3 If sharing a bedroom:

- Make a pact to say to each other as soon as waking in the morning the word 'dream' as a stimulus for remembering.
- Agree that it is OK to turn on the light during the night if you need to write a dream down.

Once I followed these instructions, I started to remember my dreams. By the end of the week the light was going on and off all during the night as Jan, my friend, and I got busy gathering our dreams. Now I could recall my dreams better. However, my understanding of them remained vague.

Jung believed that if we take the time to understand our dreams it is not difficult. If we have the attitude that dreams are complex, we are likely to design a dream analysis process equally so. If we view them as simple and straightforward, we will design a simple process that enables us to realise they are exactly that. He also said it is best to analyse our own dreams, for only we can know what certain symbols mean to us and can thus view them as 'natural phenomena which are nothing other than what they pretend to be'.

Jungian analyst James Hillman urges us to 'befriend' our dreams.

> Befriending the dream begins with a plain attempt to listen to the dream, to set down on paper or in a dream diary, in its own words just what it says. One takes special note of the feeling tone of the dream, the mood upon waking, the emotional reactions of the dreamer in the dream, the delight or fear or surprise. Befriending is the feeling approach to the dream, and so one takes care receiving the dream's feelings, as with a living person with whom we begin a friendship.

Therefore, as we would with a friend, we should spend time with our dream. We do not judge it quickly. Rather, we listen to it, and understand it from many different angles. As we become familiar with our dream, we become familiar with our inner world.

BEFRIENDING OUR DREAMS THROUGH WRITING

In January 2000, several months before starting to write this book, I attended a Dream Workshop by Rita Kryshkovski at the Council of Adult Education–*Age* Writers' Festival. She introduced me to a dream analysis writing process that incorporates many of the aspects Hillman recommends to 'befriend' our dreams. Since this time my friends, clients and I have found it a very useful technique for analysing our dreams.

If we at first make an incorrect analysis, and don't make the appropriate changes in our conscious world, it is not a big problem. As Jung explains in *Two Essays on Analytical Psychology*, 'If we have made a wrong interpretation, or if it is somehow incomplete, we may be able to see it from the next dream.' Our unconscious will keep on sending us the message in various forms, including dreams, until we hear it and incorporate its understanding into our consciousness.

I will describe the steps to the dream analysis writing process by showing you what I wrote when Rita first introduced it to me.

MY DREAM
Step 1
Write out the dream.
I am in a big house made of wood—not mine—but the house in the dream belongs to me. There is <u>water pouring into the house up in the roof</u> and parts of the <u>upper floor are collapsing</u>. I go to <u>different parts</u> of the house and everywhere parts of the

upper house are collapsing. I feel <u>panicky and frightened but not overwhelmingly so.</u>

With the collapsing parts there are brown wooden beams with white plaster board behind them. They start <u>sagging under the weight of the water. Towards the end of the dream I assume the whole house is going to collapse.</u>

Step 2

For three minutes, free-write on any topic that does not relate to the dream. Go back and underline significant words in this piece of writing and then choose one to write about for another three minutes. This free writing helps to free you from your conscious world.

Step 3

Underline words that stand out to you from your description of your dream. Now choose an underlined section that particularly stands out to you. I chose 'upper floors are collapsing', and this is what I wrote.

My old life is collapsing—but perhaps collapsing sounds too scary because this isn't how I feel about it. But now that I have written about the dream I see it as relating to how much my old life is collapsing and sometimes I do race around feeling scared especially when I go back into old ways of thinking—but perhaps ever since this dream I have felt an openness, a loosening, an ease with my life—an acceptance of just letting it flow—I TRUST—I have confidence that as long as I keep on doing what I am doing now it will find its own direction. It feels so easy like this and I only hope I can keep hold of it when Patricia, Tom and William return—there is no reason why not. I feel like the luckiest woman alive because it feels so good to be at ease in my skin. After years of not feeling so. All the changes I have made—from the outside it probably doesn't look like big changes—but from inside they have made a HUGE difference. I increasingly feel as though my life suits me. I now notice myself and notice when I am not feeling easy—and I suppose I now have pretty high standards about what I expect in my life. I don't mean money, or expensive clothes, or smart holidays—but people who I find stimulating and who are also open-hearted—control of my time—healthy food (simple food)—not too much to do—not too many people—able to remove myself from things I don't like—able to say what I want to say—not allowing others to upset me unnecessarily—not over-worrying about things. However also over these holidays I have realised I don't regret my old life—I can see how important it was for me then—to become what I am now. And to know that Pete and I can support each other in life—and leave the past behind—means a huge amount to me.

Step 4

Go back to your dream and re-write it in the third person. Make sure you spend some of the time focusing on those aspects that particularly stood out to you.

She is standing downstairs and hears water somewhere. She goes up the stairs—a little fearful of what she might find. She opens a door and is worried to see the ceiling bulging and water coming through. She races out wondering if it is about to collapse. She goes to another room and notices the same thing. She walks down the stairs—surprised that she is not more concerned about the house collapsing. Although perhaps she kids herself and is more scared than she appears.

The things that stand out for her are the rafters and plasterboard. The structures she had used for her old life are solid—but what she placed around them is flimsy. The beams are solid but also now are collapsing and what has gone first is the flimsy life—next to go will be the structures—the supports, the beams that were used to create the old life.

Once these have completely gone she will go downstairs and wait.

Step 5
Write with your non-preferred hand what you are feeling.

What were you feeling as you came down the stairs?

You were feeling scared—panicky at first—and then you calmed down.

Why did you calm down?

Because there was nothing you could do about it.

What do the beams mean?

The beams are rigid and hard and so often they will come down in a big clump.

What about the plasterboard?

With just a little stress it was soft and flaky—it collapses easily.

What's downstairs?

Downstairs there aren't any beams—there is a lot of space.

I know what this means to me. I wrote it four months ago and haven't looked at it again until typing it up now. In typing it up, I am surprised by the words. Yet I know that at the time I first wrote them, the writing process helped me recognise something important about my life. It had been a recurring dream. I thought I had already analysed it; however, once I wrote about it in this way I developed a much greater understanding of how I needed to be.

NOTICING OUR DAYDREAMS

Friends and clients are surprised when I encourage them to notice their daydreams, as well as their dreams. Daydreams are often perceived as inferior to dreaming. Yet over the last twelve years I have had several significant daydreams. They have guided me to change my personal world in order to express an until then unrecognised part of my Self. I only started noticing these daydreams as I started listening to my inner voice through meditation in my mid-thirties.

Jung says we dream and daydream because there is a message in our unconscious world that we need to bring to consciousness. Looking back at the first significant daydream that I can remember, I can now see this so clearly. Before the daydream I was already being given messages from my inner voice. I just wasn't taking much notice of them. I needed the very clear daydream to make me take action. I will recount the events leading up to it, and the actual daydream to show you what I mean.

EVENTS LEADING UP TO MY DAYDREAM

I went on a holiday with my friend, Tess, leaving my husband and three young children at home. I had the daydream as I was flying back home. Three significant things happened to me on that holiday at the Barrier Reef. First, I went scuba diving for the first time. To do this I had overcome significant fear and anxiety. After the first day of diving I leant into the wind while standing on the prow of the boat and thought to myself, 'I can do anything if I just put my mind to it.' Second, at the holiday resort there were several businessmen who, I gradually realised, appreciated being able to talk over their work issues with me. Towards the end of the holiday while talking with one of them I had this fleeting thought, 'I would be as bright if not brighter than these men. I am just as articulate, if not more so. I also probably have more formal qualifications. Why is it that they are doing more interesting, challenging, well-paid work with much greater recognition?' This was all going through my mind at a very subtle level. I also knew there were a myriad of answers to my questions.

On the last morning while having breakfast Tess turned to me and said, 'I think you will do something special with your work one day.' I was nonplussed. Tess's comment came out of the blue although it was also synchronistic with my own inner thoughts about my career. Nobody had ever indicated that I could do anything special with my work. Considering the messages I had been given as a girl and woman, I thought I was doing well to be a practising professional.

But the critical factor in getting in touch with my inner voice was the daydream I had while flying home. I put headphones on, lay back, closed my eyes and relaxed into the music. Suddenly I had a vision of myself speaking in front of a large group of people. I was dressed in a black dress and a bright jacket. It was 'corporate' dress. I hadn't ever dressed that way. As soon as I came out of this daydream I started creating a new professional life in my mind. This daydream coupled with what I had experienced while on holiday had finally made me listen to my inner voice. I came home and immediately started planning a business to consult to the corporate sector. It took eighteen months before I had made the complete transition. That didn't matter. I was focused. I finally knew what I wanted to work towards in my professional life.

This was a prophetic daydream. It was telling me about something that was going to happen. The other significant prophetic daydream I have had at midlife was when I saw in a daydream an African drum, a djembe. It was decorated with yellow and red twine and it was sitting in my living room. It took me twelve months before I came across the drum in a music shop in Melbourne. The drum has led me to regular participation and enjoyment of drumming circles, African dancing and a month in West Africa having tuition in African drumming, dance and song. It has also led me to a friendship with a beautiful Ghanaan woman called Akweley and her family. I was led to all of this by a daydream.

My daydreams have been prophetic, while my dreams have been symbolic. It might be very different for you. I didn't take note of my dreams and daydreams until midlife. Since my mid-thirties my dreams and daydreams have given me important messages about the personal world I need to create to honour an unacknowledged aspect of my Self. At a stage of such confusion as midlife I have found them an invaluable and reassuring guide.

9

Buried selves, buried energy

It is not that we have a single child within, perhaps hurt, frightened or
withdrawn in compensation, but a whole host of children, a veritable
kindergarten, including the class clown, the artist, the rebel, the
spontaneous child at one with the world.

J. Hollis, *The Middle Passage: From Misery to Meaning at Midlife*

When Jung was feeling stuck during midlife he spent hours squatting on the shores of Lake Zurich building sandcastles, playing with toy figures and shaping stones. Anybody observing him probably thought he was crazy. However, intuitively Jung knew that through play he would once again find his inner child and that this was a way he could rediscover his zest and energy for life.

All those parts of our Self that we suppressed as we grew up make up part of what Jung called our shadow. Why do we bury these parts of our Self? When we are born we are complete in our Self. Think of a baby or young child. If they are in an unrestrained environment they express in a brief period of time a range of feelings from ecstatic joy to an angry cry of hunger. They feel free to be who they are. As they develop and grow they gradually discover that different parts of themself are not acceptable. Significant others in their life give them feedback that they are doing something that isn't approved of. Perhaps they notice a frown on Daddy's face when they scream with delight, or a displeased look from their kindergarten teacher when they shout angrily at a friend who has taken their favourite toy. As they get the message that certain aspects of themself aren't acceptable to others, they bury these parts deep inside.

It is likely that as children we were often discouraged by parents, teachers and significant others from expressing our feelings. They sent us messages that encouraged us to bury much of our anger, sadness, hurt, fear, vulnerability, love, passion and even joy. And as we became teenagers we were encouraged to bury our sexuality and sensuality as well. In many ways we were sanitised. These feelings and parts of our Self don't disappear. They are still inside us and they are important.

A useful way of seeing these buried parts of our Self is as energy patterns that are deep inside us. This buried energy can have all sorts of effects on our life. First, because part of our life energy is buried, we don't realise our full potential for vitality. Second, this buried energy can affect us physically, by creating blockages in our body, leading to illness and other common concerns, such as excess weight. Third, the buried selves, the buried energy patterns can be triggered off by people or things in our environment, making us react in an emotionally inappropriate and uncharacteristic way.

I will give a personal example to illustrate this third point. As long as I can remember I have had a strong fear of anger and angry people. When somebody expresses anger, even when I can see it is reasonable, my stomach tenses up and I want to run a mile. I grew up in a home where expressing anger was taboo. At times it was expressed, but usually in an explosive, venting way with little space for constructive discussion. I never saw my mother express anger. From my first day of school, one teacher in particular expressed anger towards me and this continued for several years. So, like many people, I have grown up with an unnatural fear of anger. Perhaps I should say I *had* an unnatural fear of anger because I do think I am getting better at dealing with it. In the last couple of years I have taken steps to express anger appropriately and have been surprised when my world doesn't fall apart, and by the rush of energy through my body. I have also found that when others express anger to me I am gradually learning to remain calm, and to endeavour to reflect back an understanding of why they are feeling that way.

Like all of us, during my life I have been in situations where I have had good reason to feel angry. Rather than expressing it—believing it was wrong, dangerous or unfair to do so— I have held it inside myself. This buried energy from unexpressed anger has weighed me down so much that I have felt lethargic and even depressed. And this is often what depression is; unexpressed anger turned in on oneself. In contrast, when acknowledged and constructively channelled, anger can be an important stimulus for needed change.

Expressing or experiencing anger from another is still not easy for me, but as I am now conscious of it I am gradually learning to change my response. This part of me is no longer buried. I am learning to express it constructively. I am learning not to run away when others express it to me. At times my children will turn to me in surprise and say, 'Mum, you sound angry!' Instead of apologising, as once I would have, I now say,

'Yes, I am angry,' knowing it is all right for me to feel that way as long as I express it constructively.

Every disowned part of our Self buried in our unconscious has an equal and opposite energy in our conscious. For example, when I disowned my anger I considered myself to be a gentle, peace-making woman. The more I saw myself this way, the more I kept my anger buried. Eventually through counselling, reading and reflection, I have made conscious to myself that I am both these things. I am gradually gaining a more balanced attitude to these qualities in both myself and others.

Each of us will have different, significant selves that have been buried. Which ones have been buried will be dependent mostly on our upbringing. For each of us there are usually some key buried selves which once released, allow others to easily follow. What do you think yours might be? How might you be able to release them? During midlife transition I have found a variety of ways to make contact with some of my buried little girls, the buried parts of my Self. And as I have in turn uncovered them my zest and energy for life has increased.

At my fortieth birthday my vulnerable self was finally out in the open. A few people had seen glimpses of her over the years and she had been popping out more and more at unexpected times. However, mostly she had been buried deep inside me. A recurring saying of my father's was 'Stiff upper lip'. He even said it to us as my mother's hearse drove past. He was steeped in the Anglo-Saxon tradition of not showing emotions, especially sad, angry and vulnerable ones. Messages sent to me throughout my childhood made me think, 'Don't feel too much or too deeply. It is dangerous to do so.'

I learnt at a young age to bury strong feelings and subsequent parts of my Self as a way of seeking my father's and significant others' approval. At my fortieth birthday in front of friends and family I was not my usual sociable, chatty, happy self. It was as though my vulnerable self had been buried for so long it was now saying to me, 'I'm here. Notice me. I'm an important part of you.' At the time I felt embarrassed about how I was. However, no matter how much I tried I couldn't be any other way. After my fortieth birthday I knew I had blown my cover. I had to get some help to understand this part of me.

One of our primary needs as children is to be able to experience and express our feelings. In turn we need another to understand how we are feeling without trying to suppress or change them. If as a child we can express to our parents or significant others our feelings of anger, sadness, joy and love and have them say or acknowledge in body language, 'Yes, I understand and accept how you feel', we learn to understand and accept those parts of our Self.

After my fortieth birthday I spent several years with a counsellor who did exactly this. He provided the space for me to explore a range of feelings and through his acknowledgment of them he helped me to know and finally accept them in myself. In many ways an effective counsellor takes us back and re-parents us appropriately by allowing us to express all those feelings we have buried. At first he helped me to know and accept my feelings of vulnerability. Once I did this, all the other little girls came skipping out. At the same time my personal wellbeing and energy for life increased.

I no longer feel embarrassed about my feelings. I now know all of them are an important part of me. For example, these days when I feel vulnerable, I stop and notice and look at what is happening in my life to make me feel this way. I look after this part of myself. I have found that once I experienced and subsequently accepted my feelings they no longer seemed as scary as they used to.

At midlife we need to start reclaiming these buried parts of our Self if we are to move towards individuation. And as we do this we will also reclaim energy that is buried deep inside us. It is a time to ask: 'What little girls are buried inside me?' For no matter what obligations we have to work, family and friends, we have an obligation to ourselves and to those forgotten little girls inside us.

As well as counselling, I have found attending a variety of workshops, classes and festivals a most enjoyable way of discovering different parts of myself. For example, I first felt the release of a joyful, free dancing little girl inside me at a Soul Dance workshop several years ago. We were asked to move freely around the room to music. I was suddenly a little girl again. I started to cry for that little girl who had rarely, if ever, felt the wonder of moving freely to music. I kept on moving as I cried. I didn't want to stop. Since that time, I have often created the opportunity to dance freely. I put on music at home and dance around our back room or in my bedroom. I also go out with friends where there is suitable music to freely dance. Now I am a woman dancing. Contacting that little girl in me helped me to reclaim a part of myself that I needed to enjoy as a woman. And as I do this I also tap into a vital energy source.

One Sunday morning a couple of years ago I was running around the botanical gardens with a woman I had just met that morning. A mutual acquaintance was running ahead of us. As we ran, we chatted. I mentioned that the night before, as I had the house to myself, I put on music and danced for three hours. I explained that as I warmed up I gradually shed clothes and inhibitions and had a ball. My running partner said nothing and as I ran I thought, 'Oh well, she probably thinks I'm a bit odd.' We kept on running. When we were having coffee afterwards she turned to me and said, 'You know, I did the same thing.' At first I didn't know what she was talking about, then she explained that she had also spent the night before at home dancing. I suddenly had a vision of women all around Melbourne dancing in their homes. What a wonderful thought!

The next evening I was telling my children the story when one of my sons said, 'How sad.' I realised he was feeling sad that I had no one to dance with. I explained to him that it wasn't sad at all. Far from it. It was joyous. I knew I could dance whenever I wanted to. I also thought to myself, I can find the free spirited, joyous, sensuous parts of myself, with all the energy that comes with them.

So my suggestion is to take advantage of all the adult and community workshops and classes to help make contact with your lost little girls. You might need to explore for quite a while like I did. For example, I attended watercolour painting classes for eighteen months before finally accepting it wasn't for me. I tried many different forms of dance before recognising that it was free form dancing to African drums which most centred me. I tried gospel singing for several months before deciding I preferred other types of singing. I started writing classes and was amazed at the energy and passion released from inside me once I was being taught in a way that suited me. All of these activities freed me up to start exploring myself. However, if at this stage it seems like too big a step to attend these sorts of classes, consider reading books on various subjects to see which draw your energy and attention.

It is so important to rediscover our buried selves and allow them to express themselves. As we discover the true feelings and needs of our little girls and begin to nurture and care for them consciously and effectively, we find that most of our old, rigid defence systems are no longer necessary, and we begin to relax and let go. And as we do, we come alive and bring emotional depth and authenticity, spontaneity and joy into our life.

10

Gathering up your projections

*. . . because projections are unconscious, they appear on persons in
the immediate environment, mostly in the form of abnormal over- or
under-valuations which provoke misunderstandings, quarrels,
fanatacisms, rumours, suspicions, prejudices.*

C.G. Jung, *Two Essays on Analytical Psychology*

In the last chapter I talked about how as we grow up, various
parts of our Self get buried deep inside us. This is because for
one reason or another we saw these parts of us as unacceptable.
A most effective way at midlife to uncover these buried parts of
our Self is to notice, and then gather up our projections.

Projection occurs when a vital part of our Self that we have
buried, is activated by another's perceived behaviour. When we
project we see that part outside of our Self, as if it belongs to
someone else and has nothing to do with us. There is something
thing in that person that triggers our projection. It is an
unconscious process of the psyche. If we were conscious of that
aspect in ourselves we could not project it because only unconscious aspects of our personality are projected.

Projection is a defence mechanism we use all our life.
It starts when we are young as a way of coping with our

awesome, outer world. When we were overwhelmed by feelings we couldn't manage, we projected them onto our primary love object, usually our mother. If she was capable of understanding and accepting our feelings without her own psyche being too disturbed, she could contain the feelings for us, and behave in a way towards us that made the difficult feelings more acceptable to us. We could then take them back in a form that we could manage better and consciously claim as part of our Self. For example, if your child gets irrationally angry with you and you are able to respond calmly and rationally, her own feelings will be reflected back to her and she will be able to own them. I will give a very simple example from my own life. When my daughter first started school she often used to come out at the end of the day and kick me. This was such an out of character behaviour for her I made little comment except to say occasionally, 'You're feeling angry about something.' Soon her kicking stopped and over time she talked about many of the things happening at school that she found difficult.

Later in life we also project onto our partner, children, friends and work colleagues. We can also project onto institutions such as our place of work, or onto objects, such as works of art. If at midlife we are to move ourselves towards wholeness, towards individuation, we need to start collecting up these parts of our Self that we have projected.

So next time you have a strong reaction to someone else, don't automatically assume the qualities you are responding to are in them. More than likely your feelings are telling you something about yourself that you as yet don't consciously acknowledge. Take notice when you say to yourself, 'I can't stand her arrogance', 'He's absolutely wonderful', 'Gosh, she's so talented'.

This may be a golden opportunity for you to learn more about yourself.

Jung said our psyche is made up of pairs of opposites such as happy versus sad, male versus female, loyal versus disloyal. He said that each part of a pair needs its opposite to exist. For example, happy would not mean anything unless we also knew what we mean by sad. Because each opposite element assumes the other, all are a valuable and necessary part of our Self.

Our psyche is divided into the conscious and unconscious and they work together to keep the psyche balanced. As we mature, if our conscious attitude—that part of our Self we know and accept—is too one-sided, its opposite will manifest in the unconscious to counteract the imbalance. We may experience this unconscious component internally in dreams and visual images. However, if the imbalance gets too great we will project it externally onto something or someone in our environment. For example, a woman who is overly confident is likely to have an equally exaggerated but unconscious sense of lack of confidence. She may frequently have strong, negative feelings towards people she perceives as lacking in confidence. She may respond negatively when colleagues express their vulnerability, or when her children display lack of confidence in themselves. In both these cases she is rejecting in others an unconscious, unacknowledged part of herself. These others may or may not possess her disowned attribute.

This is not to say that all strong reactions to another are projection. A person's behaviour may warrant our reaction. Sometimes people around us do things that understandably make us feel strong emotions. However, often they are simply a hook on which we can hang our projections. When there is a positive projection we are attracted to a person. This often accounts for why people will instantly fall in love with another. They are actually falling in love with a projected attribute of themselves. For is it possible to love someone you don't even know? When there is a negative projection we are repelled by a person. This can be seen when we experience an immediate dislike for a person on first meeting.

Usually, projections only work temporarily. If a person fails to notice themself in the projection, it will eventually lead them into trouble. For example, a woman who always perceives herself as competent eventually will be faced with a situation where she isn't competent. Life is providing her with an experience to make conscious this unconscious part of her Self. If she continues to ignore this unconscious part of her Self, her judgment may be severely impaired and disaster could follow. Perhaps she may be competent in her day-to-day job but have very poor public speaking skills. If when she is asked to give a talk to clients, she doesn't recognise and remedy her lack of skills, she may give her speech incompetently, and only afterwards realise how she has let herself down. If she does this she will be making conscious an until now unconscious part of her Self. Of course, she may find others to blame for the botched up job, still not willing to look at her own incompetence, and thus still projecting this unconscious part of her Self.

When we first learn about projection we often only think about projecting negative aspects of our Self. However, this is not true. We also project our own 'gold'. For example, I have admired writers all my life, and I now realise that this has been an important part of my Self which I have projected onto others. It is not only proficient writers I have admired. Nearly everybody I know I have regarded as a good writer. When others told me I could write well, I didn't hear them. It took a huge amount of personal effort, and painful soul searching to start taking back this projection. And now I find I judge others' writing with a much more balanced eye.

Is there a particular group you admire? Perhaps you admire artists, sculptors, musicians, landscape gardeners or photographers. Could this be telling you something about your Self that you are not acknowledging?

Noticing projections of positive attributes of ourselves, although still not easy to do, is of course pleasing to talk about afterwards. It's nice to reclaim such a special part of our Self. However, with those negative attributes we have projected onto others—perhaps mistrustful, egocentric, dishonest, aloof, disloyal—it is not so comfortable to think about reclaiming these parts of our Self. We have been brought up to believe such bad things about these attributes that when we have seen them in ourselves, we have quickly pushed them into our unconscious. When there is too great an imbalance and the pressure gets too much, this aspect of ourselves will get pushed to the surface and projected onto someone or something else. Eventually something will happen to encourage us to accept our projection.

Women at midlife today are more likely to have an under-inflated psyche than an over-inflated one. We have been encouraged to disown our own skills and knowledge. We have often been trained to denigrate ourselves. I continually see women disown their competence both at work and in their personal lives. When they do something well, they attribute it to luck or perhaps to another person. If they continue to only be conscious of areas in which they are incompetent, while not acknowledging their talents, skills and knowledge, their self-esteem will be low. It is very likely that their professional and personal life will be restricted and unfulfilled. Women can make dramatic, positive changes to their lives by being encouraged to own their competence. For example, when congratulated for a job well done say, 'Thank you.' This is the assertive response—in contrast to the usual, 'Oh it was nothing. Anybody could have done it.'

How can we gather in our projections so we can become more complete in our Self? An important step is to start noticing ourselves—our thoughts, our behaviours, our conversations. To keep our psyche in some equilibrium takes a fair bit of vigilance, and in many ways it is impossible to maintain complete balance. However, if we are continually overreacting, either positively or negatively to other people or situations, this could indicate a projection.

We can become aware of the following stages and notice them when they occur in our life as a way of gathering up our projections:

1 We are convinced that something from our unconscious is actually part of our outer world.
2 We gradually recognise and acknowledge a discrepancy between the projected image and what we find to be true.
3 We conclude that for some reason our original judgment was wrong.
4 We search for the origin of the projection within ourselves.

For example, we perceive a friend as distrustful. Eventually we notice, through others' comments about our friend or through our own observations, that our friend is mostly trusting. We wonder why we perceived our friend in a distorted way. We realise after much soul searching that it is actually an aspect of ourself that we have not wanted to own. That is, at times we are distrustful.

This final step, the search for the source of the projection in oneself and the meaning of this projection may be a painful one. However, it is a vital step for us all if we are to increase knowledge of our Self.

11

Finding your joyful, passionate and creative self

In the middle passage we are invited to find our passion.
It is an imperative to find that which draws us so deeply into our life
and our own nature that it hurts, for that experience transforms us.

J. Hollis, *The Middle Passage: From Misery to Meaning at Midlife*

I hadn't seen Margie for several years. We exchanged the usual hello and how are you. She then asked me about my children. After answering, I was about to ask after hers when I thought, not for the first time, 'Why do we women so often ask each other about our children instead of asking about each other?' I hesitated and then asked, 'And how about you Margie? What's happening in your life?'

With that, Margie's face lit up. 'I'm painting! I've just had my first solo exhibition.'

Margie described to me how one day at breakfast she turned to her husband and said, 'Now that the children are older, what am I going to do with my life?' and he replied, 'Why don't you go back to Art School?'

At the first class Margie's teacher turned to her and said, 'Why are you here? You can paint already.'

In the middle of the men's clothes shop Margie started to describe to me the tightness in her stomach, and then the energy and passion released inside her as she began to paint again. Waking up early each morning full of energy, she couldn't wait to start another day of painting.

'I get butterflies in my stomach until I start to paint. There is all this stuff inside me I just want to get out onto the canvas.'

Margie says she has friends who seem to be dying inside. They ask, 'Where do you get all your energy from?'

And Margie and I share the knowledge that when you are involved passionately in a creative pursuit—whether it be painting, writing, sculpting, gardening or some other all-consuming interest—you have the same energy for yourself and your passion as you would for a lover.

In his essay 'The Creative Moment', Robert Dessaix compares the moment of creativity with the moment of falling in love.

LET US CAST OUR MINDS BACK: when we fall in love, we're aware that not only something has happened, but that what has happened is, not so much unconnected with our will and knowledge, as beyond will and knowledge. It's not being in love I have in mind here, not loving somebody. What I want to focus on is that astounding instant when you think to yourself, 'Good grief, I've been zapped. I've just fallen in love!'

Creativity is about something out there connecting with something inside ourself. This connection is similar to falling in love with another; something within that person out there connects with something inside us.

Margie's experience was very similar to mine when my words first flowed as I started writing this book. In those first few weeks I could think of little else but my writing. I had an excited energy inside me. I lost weight. I wanted to spend as much time as possible with my writing. I felt protective when somebody wanted to come between us. I had previously read Robert Dessaix's essay and during those early weeks I was very aware that my feelings and responses were similar to those magical and at times disturbing reactions I had felt when falling in love with another.

Why are our feelings in the creative moment so similar to that moment of falling in love? I believe it is because we are falling in love with part of our Self. I had started nurturing my writing self by going to writing classes and writing festivals and making time for writing at home. However, it wasn't until I started to trust my writing self that my writing started to flow. It was then that we truly connected as I started to write this book. As I fell more in love with my writing self I knew I never wanted it to leave me. I wanted to look after it, make room for it, and nurture this part of my Self for the rest of my life.

And, of course, the wonderful thing about finding our own love within our Self is that nobody can take it away from us unless we let them. Our creativity belongs to us. It is not like a lover who might decide they wish to leave us.

Robert Dessaix goes on to say that he doesn't believe creativity is something that can be taught: '. . . it's something that happens—something I can put myself in the way of . . .'

We can take ourselves to classes, we can buy paper, pens, paints and paint brushes, chunks of clay and a potter's wheel, cameras and film and thus 'put ourselves in the way of' it. However, something out there has to connect with something inside ourselves to stimulate that inner creativity. Something out there has to stir our passions, our inner Self.

When I ask clients who are at midlife if there is something they want to make time for, they almost inevitably mention a creative activity such as painting, writing, photography or playing a musical instrument. However, they give the impression they have to change their whole lifestyle to honour their creativity. Certainly we have to make time for it, but we don't have to give up our day job, or significantly change our lifestyle, to start loving our creative self.

THE ARTIST'S WAY

A wonderful resource for discovering and recovering our creative self is Julia Cameron's book *The Artist's Way*. In this book she describes the process she uses in her workshops to assist people to 'put themselves in the way of' their creativity. She states:

> I teach people to let themselves be creative . . . No matter what your age or your life path, whether making art is your career or your hobby or your day dream, it is not too late, or too egotistical or too selfish or too silly to work on your creativity.

She goes on to say:

> . . . through my experience—and that of countless others that I have shared—I have come to believe that creativity is our true nature, that blocks are an unnatural thwarting of a process of making spiritual contact to be both simple and straightforward.

I agree. If we observe anyone who is following their passion through creative pursuits we see that is when they are truly happy; that is when they are in love with life; that is when they have passion in their life.

PUTTING OURSELF IN THE WAY OF OUR CREATIVITY

It takes time to open up to our creativity. And that time has to be free of many of the distractions we so often allow to take over our lives. Over the last few years I have practised many of the suggestions made in *The Artist's Way*. I was carrying out many of them as a means to understand myself better. However, I hadn't realised then that I was also structuring a personal environment to put myself in the way of my creativity.

In my experience the creative process is similar to the movement of a steam train. It takes a tremendous amount of personal energy to get the wheels moving, and they move very slowly at first. If in these early stages something gets in the way, such as some discouraging feedback, the train easily stops in its tracks. However, once it has got up full steam it takes a lot for something to stop it. I also found getting my steam train of creativity moving was very painful at first. To me it was a bit like giving birth. However, once I confidently held my 'writing baby' in my heart it has mostly been joy since.

When I started writing I had to focus much of my time and energy on it. I said 'no' to friends and activities. I cut back my work and social life to have enough steam for my writing. Now that my writing is well established I am flexible about when and where I write. However, if you have a creative project you would like to begin, I suggest you say 'no' to as many distractions as possible, so you can build up steam to move forward with it.

MORNING PAGES

In *The Artist's Way*, Julia Cameron suggests that one of the most effective ways of 'putting yourself in the way of your creativity' is to write morning pages. Whether you are a potter, a sculptor, writer, artist, playwright, movie director, she says, 'the morning pages are the primary tool of creative recovery'.

You create 'morning pages' by writing three foolscap pages when you first wake up in the morning. When writing you don't use grammar and you don't stop writing until you have filled up three pages. When I can't think what to write, I sometimes write repeatedly 'I wonder' or sometimes just 'blah, blah, blah' depending on my mood. The important thing is to keep my pen moving. Sometimes I will write absolute rubbish and that's fine because the morning pages are for me, nobody else. Other times, I slip down into a place where I discover feelings and thoughts I hadn't consciously been aware of.

THE ARTIST'S DATE

The next step encouraged in *The Artist's Way* is for us to create a block of time in our week, as little as two hours, especially put aside to develop our creative self. This doesn't mean you have to pick up a paintbrush and start painting during this time. It might mean a stroll in your favourite gardens. Or listening to your favourite music. Perhaps dancing around your bedroom. It is something that stimulates your inner being. It is also something you do alone for spending time in solitude is essential to nurture your creative self. Listen to your inner voice to hear how your creative self is responding to these dates. Perhaps you are choosing activities that you think should please it but on consideration you realise they are not. For example, you have always attended the opera thinking this was nourishing you and you realise it is not the case anymore. You now realise that to nourish your creative self you like to be more actively involved.

You may be surprised to find how difficult it is at first to give yourself permission to take this time out for your creative self.

Ideas in other chapters, especially Chapters 16, 17 and 18 give you strategies to help you make this time available.

Julia Cameron suggests that the morning pages evoke questions and concerns, and the artist's date is a time when we are likely to come up with solutions to these concerns. The artist's date makes sure we give attention to our creative self, as we would a loved one. We nourish and nurture it and let it know that it is important to us.

Nurturing our creative self

When we are creating we are creating from inside ourselves. If we don't replenish this inner world we can easily get depleted. Recently I heard a well-known writer speak. She described how she had spent eighteen hours a day writing her most recent book and sometimes forgot to eat. I was sitting in the front row with a friend and we could see this writer clearly. Her face was gaunt and she looked very fragile.

We have all heard stories of 'creatives' gradually destroying themselves. It is often assumed that this is an aspect of being creative. When creating from our inner world it is important to keep in contact with our outer, physical needs. As well as being physically nourished, we need to continue to feed our soul, in whatever form that takes. This is why once our creativity starts flowing we still need to take ourselves on the 'artist's date'. I mention this because from my own experience it is easy to forget our other world, when we first fall in love with our creative self. When I started writing this book, for several weeks I stopped walking my dog, visiting our Botanical Gardens and listening to music. Gradually I put these back into my life and I know they nourish me as I continue to write with ease.

Recently I completed a writing workshop where the facilitator made writing sound like such a bleak, driven experience that if I had not already been writing I could have been put off it forever. She encouraged us to set a timetable for our writing, a suggestion I don't necessarily agree with. Some 'creatives' of a certain personality type will be stifled by a timetable, others will benefit from it. Despite saying this, I do not want to give the impression that creativity doesn't require discipline. As Julia Cameron points out:

> One of the great misconceptions about the artistic life is that it entails great swathes of aimlessness. The truth is that a creative life involves great swathes of attention.

I do give my writing a lot of attention; however, from one day to the next I am not sure how, when, what or where I will be writing. Some 'creatives' couldn't operate this way. I can. The answer is that we are all different. It is important for us to think creatively about how to get our own creativity going. We assist ourselves by thinking of ways to nurture ourselves during the creative process.

For example, at no time did the workshop facilitator mention creating the right sort of environment to encourage writing to flow. This might not have been important for her. For me it is vital. I have favourite places I write from depending on my mood. In the early morning I sit in an armchair in my bedroom, sipping hazelnut-flavoured coffee, and thinking about how I might creatively approach the next chapter. I also enjoy tapping in to my creativity while writing in coffee shops and our Botanical Gardens. I do spend time at my computer in my study, although I do not find my study to be a place that stimulates my senses to be creative. So I mainly do word processing there. As I write I will also often have classical music playing, in winter the heater near me, and my golden retriever, Bertie, and my cat, Benji for company. These all nurture my Self and my creativity as I write.

NOTICE CREATIVE MOMENTS

When I first started focusing on my writing seriously, I noticed that certain activities resulted in a train of thought that once captured on paper would be 'good' writing. One of these times was in the shower. To capture this writing I set up my laptop in my bedroom and switched it on before hopping into the shower. Often after showering I would quickly dry myself and sit down in front of my laptop. Half an hour later I would still be tapping away with a towel draped around me, all the words that had been tumbling through my head while in the shower now recorded.

PROTECTING OUR CREATIVE SELF

Once your creativity is flowing, make sure you protect your creative self. For many of us it is like a young child and very fragile. During my early days of exploring my creativity there were a couple of people in my life who unintentionally sent me the message that they didn't believe in my ability to be creative. At this stage I limited my contact with them, or certainly didn't talk about my creative pursuits with them. As much as possible I discussed my 'dreams' with people who gave me support in believing in my burgeoning creative self. Now that I have more confidence I share with greater ease my writing, my drumming and my 'creative' dancing and singing with friends and family. I also continue to 'protect' my creativity and remain vigilant against discouragement from others. As my creative self matures, I assume this vigilance will not be so necessary.

12

Creating personal mandalas for healing and wholeness

I sketched every morning in a notebook a small circular drawing,

a mandala, which seemed to correspond to my inner situation

at the time . . . only gradually did I discover what the mandala really

is; . . . the Self, the wholeness of the personality, which if all goes well

is harmonious . . .

C. G. Jung, *Memories, Dreams and Reflections*

In previous chapters we have explored the use of meditation, storytelling and dream analysis to tap into the unconscious. Jung found, as had others before him, that another way to tap into the unconscious, and thus the Self, is to create a personal mandala.

I saw a mandala in a dream about nine months before starting this book. At the time I wasn't sure what it was. I started reading about mandalas. I had created a large, round bare patch in my native garden eighteen months previously. When people asked me what it was for, I would reply, 'I'm not sure, but I know the answer will come.' After the dream, I decided it was telling me to build a brick mandala there. I made plans but as yet have not built it. Six months ago I created a personal mandala at a workshop at a Healing Arts Festival. I have become fascinated with mandalas and have only now started to understand and explore their connection to healing and wholeness.

Jung introduced the idea of the mandala to modern psychology. He adopted the Sanskrit word 'mandala' to describe the circular drawings he became fascinated with at the age of 38. He had recently quit his university post and was at a time of transition. As he spent time writing in his journal he simply followed an inner impulse and started to sketch circular designs in it. Jung noticed that the drawings changed as his mood changed. Through reading he realised that similar drawings are found in the art of virtually all cultures. These drawings used a perfectly balanced circle or square, in which the midpoint is given particularly great importance. They are found in Ancient rock carvings in Africa, Europe and North America. Tibetans use mandalas to serve as a visual aid to meditation. There are wonderful examples of mandalas in Gothic cathedrals in Europe, such as those I saw in Chartres Cathedral in France.

In *Memories, Dreams and Reflections* Jung wrote:

> I was being compelled to go through this process of the un-conscious. I had to let myself be carried along by the current, without a notion of where it would lead me. When I began drawing the mandalas, however, I saw that everything, all the paths I had been following, all the steps I had taken, were leading back to a single point—namely, to the mid-point. It became increasingly plain to me that the mandala is the centre. It is the exponent of all paths. It is the path to the centre, to individuation.

The spontaneous appearance of a mandala in dreams, day-dreams and artwork indicates that individuation is taking place. When we create a personal mandala, we represent symbolically who we are at that time, and from my experience there can be significant insight gained, with a concurrent release of inner tension.

In *Mandala Symbolism* Jung explains:

> The fact that images of this kind have under certain circum-
> stances a considerable therapeutic effect on their authors is
> empirically proved and also readily understandable, in that they
> often represent very bold attempts to see and put together
> apparently irreconcilable opposites and bridge over apparently
> hopeless splits. Even the mere attempt in this direction usually
> has a healing effect . . .

Jung discovered that drawing, painting and dreaming mandalas is a natural part of the individuation process. They tended to appear at times of psychic confusion, such as midlife transition. He encouraged his patients to give free rein to their imagination and create mandalas spontaneously, without a predetermined pattern in mind.

In the rest of this chapter I explain a mandala drawing process. To do this I have drawn on my experience while attending a mandala workshop called 'The Mandala: Drawing Towards Wholeness', run by Glenda Lehmann at the Council of Adult Education. I have also drawn on information in Susanne Fincher's informative book, *Creating Mandalas for Insight, Healing and Self-Expression*.

A MANDALA DRAWING PROCESS

The materials supplied to us by Glenda were:

- several large pieces of white drawing paper;
- oil pastels, felt-tip pens and colouring pencils;

- a paper plate (not necessary—most of us drew our circles by hand);
- a pen or pencil; and
- an optional ruler, compass and notebook.

Step 1

Ensure you have a quiet, spacious area where you will not be interrupted for at least an hour if you are working alone, or two hours if you are working in a group. Design a ritual for the beginning, such as silence, relaxation music, or the burning of incense and candles. This helps to create a reflective, tranquil atmosphere.

Step 2

Place your materials in front of you, on the floor or on any flat surface. Ensure you can be comfortable as you work.

Step 3

Begin to relax your mind to enhance creativity. Clear it of any concerns. Close you eyes and focus on your breathing. Scan your body for any tension and as you exhale visualise it leaving your body.

Step 4

While creating your mandala it is best to suspend all thought and judgment and to work as intuitively as possible. Look within and notice any forms, shapes or colours. They may come as an internal visual image or they may present more as an idea. If nothing comes to you, be guided by your intuition. Start your mandala.

Step 5

Choose suitable pastels, felt-tip pens or coloured pencils as you work. You can begin anywhere. Remember there is no right or wrong way to make your mandala. Fill in your circle with whatever shapes and colours come to mind. When you sense that your mandala is finished go on to the next step.

Step 6

Spend time with your mandala. Turn it around until you sense that it is the right way up. Place a small 't' on the top right-hand corner.

Step 7

Put the date on your mandala. If you do several mandalas over an extended period of time you will be able to go back and look for meaning and patterns in the sequence. At times you will want to do more than one mandala on the same day. If you do, remember to number them in sequence, as well as including the date.

Step 8

Place your mandala in front of you. Make sure that the 't' is at the top. If you are working with others, exchange mandalas and spend a couple of minutes looking at another's. In turn, you can each hold the other person's mandala up and give feedback about what you perceive. Write words next to the mandala to clarify feedback to the other person. Spend time in the group focusing and enjoying each other's mandala. If you are working alone, write down for yourself any associations that come to mind as you look at your mandala.

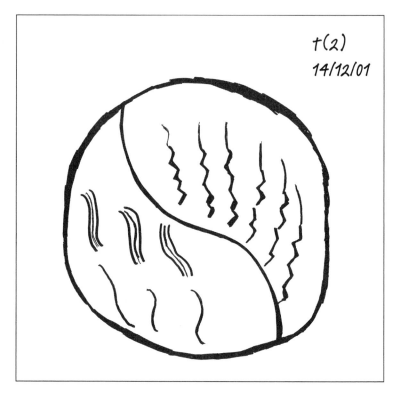

My mandala from Glenda's workshop

You can end the process here. If you want to spend more time with your mandala you could:

- give it a title, with as little thought as possible;
- note the colours you have used to create your mandala, especially the colour you used to draw the circle and the colours inside the circle;
- write down any associations you have with any of these colours;
- note the different shapes in your mandala and any associations that come to mind; and
- count the number of times a particular shape is drawn.

Read through your responses to the above and look for patterns and meaning. Can you perceive a central theme for your mandala? Write it down.

I went along to Glenda's mandala workshop thinking I might find it interesting, given the focus of my book. I was surprised, however, by significant moments of insight and emotional release during the workshop and feelings of tranquillity that lasted for several days afterwards. From my experience of this workshop I believe one of the key factors in the whole process is creating an appropriate space and atmosphere before the mandala drawing commences. Glenda spent about half an hour working with us to create a peaceful, relaxing and trusting environment. And although we knew our time was limited, she in no way made us feel rushed. Her calm, encouraging manner assisted the process immensely.

If you would like to explore the drawing of mandalas for Self understanding and healing, you can easily adapt the above process to use at home by yourself, or with a small group of friends. Otherwise I highly recommend looking for a workshop run by a skilled facilitator. Good luck!

13

Using Jung's psychological types to explain uncharacteristic behaviour at midlife

If used with care, psychological type codes can serve
as an organising principle for helping people examine, and
ultimately make sense of their midlife experiences.

Eleanor Corlett & Nancy Millner, *Navigating Midlife*

From our earliest years we all use some personal system for understanding people. When young, most of us learnt to use our own reactions to what we felt and observed as a basis for explaining our own and others' behaviour. I remember sitting in the car with my sister, Judy, when young and watching the people walk by. From what we observed we would try and guess their life story. I have automatically done this all my life.

Personality theories studied by psychologists attempt to organise observations of people by providing some kind of underlying framework for classifying and describing behaviour. Often these theories are cumbersome and use language and concepts that are difficult to understand. In contrast, psychological type theory as developed by Jung is accessible for an everyday understanding of personality. It was formulated to describe and explain normal behavioural variations among 'normal' people. Even though the style and language Jung used to describe his system can be confusing, Katharine Briggs and Isabel Briggs Myers, have provided an easily understandable interpretation of Jung's original work with their development of the Myers-Briggs Type Indicator (MBTI).

I first came across the MBTI twelve years ago when I started my business as a consultant. Just before this change in career direction I had been considering giving up psychology and training as a naturopath. Although I had enjoyed my ten years as an educational psychologist, I often felt under-challenged by the work. I also felt frustrated that as a psychologist I had not come across any theory that consistently assisted me in understanding myself or my clients. In many ways I was feeling professionally inadequate. I had been well trained and clients were satisfied; however, I felt there was something missing.

It was suggested to me that I learn to use the MBTI as it would be useful in my work as a consultant. I remember sitting in the four-day seminar in absolute wonder. After validating my own personality type, so much about myself that had bewildered me became clear. I could see why I had been under-stimulated by my previous work. My personality type indicated that for me 'life is a creative adventure full of exciting possibilities'. Life as a consultant was much more likely to offer me this than my previous work.

I had been led to the idea of starting my own business as a consultant through a daydream. In those days it had seemed a pretty shaky indicator. My understanding of my own personality type was now affirming my decision. The MBTI affirmed me in many other ways also. It helped me understand why I was different from others, especially those in my family. When young I had often wanted to be like my older sister, Judy, especially at school. She was always well organised, conscientious and non-questioning of the status quo. When young I was often disorganised, always wondering 'Why?', and with 'my head in the clouds'. I was always getting into trouble at school. I now understood why we were naturally so different. Certainly I had benefited from growing up beside her as it helped me to develop those areas that didn't come naturally to me. However I now understood I would never be able to do with the same ease those things Judy was naturally good at, no matter how much I practised. She had her preferred way of living, and I had mine. It was clear to me I needed to start validating my strengths more. In the work context, being a consultant would do this. Abilities I had taken for granted I now realised were strengths which I should acknowledge, value and build on. I also realised that others had their own areas of strength. At last I had a theory and framework to help me understand myself and others.

In the past twelve years I have administered the MBTI to about 800 people in both group and individual settings. I have used it for personal development, team development, leadership development, management development, change management, career transition and vocational counselling. Often clients have shown the same sense of wonder that I did on that first day as they read a description that reflects back to them who they are.

The MBTI has an amazing history. Isabel Briggs, living in the United States early last century, recognised through her observation of others that people's behaviour fell into certain patterns. She wasn't a psychologist or a sociologist, but her father was a university professor so she had access to research facilities and groups. After developing her insights she discovered that Jung, in Switzerland, had come up with a similar understanding of people's behaviour. Jung said that although our behaviour seems random, it is not at all. Once we know what to look for we can see that we all have a preferred way of doing things. He said that we are born with a certain personality type and how well this develops depends on our environment. Some environments will encourage development of our true type, others will discourage it.

The MBTI was researched for 30 years before being made available for general use through trained professionals. In a study that asked people to evaluate a number of personality instruments (Druckman & Bjork, 1991), the majority identified the MBTI as providing the most insights and as having the greatest impact on their behaviour and decisions. When a client comes for individual counselling I don't always use the MBTI; however, when we are in transition and questioning ourselves and our world it assists us enormously to have a clearer understanding of our own personality type.

For those of you who as yet have not learnt about personality type theory, I will give a simple explanation as it is such a valuable understanding. However, there is no way I can do it justice in this chapter. Whole books are written about different applications of type. I will do the best I can to give you enough understanding to hopefully entice you to learn more about it from a qualified practitioner. As a further introduction I suggest you read *Gifts Differing* by Isabel Briggs Myers and Peter Myers.

PERSONALITY TYPE THEORY

Personality type theory hinges on the idea that we all have a preferred way of doing things, very similar to our preference for writing with one hand over another. We can write with both hands but with our preferred hand it is easier, our writing flows and we are competent. Similarly, in life, if we know our personality type and thus our preferences and we structure our life around using these preferences, most of the time our life and the way we go about doing the things within it will seem easy, will flow and we will feel competent.

The MBTI focuses on four paired preferences. The first pair are opposite attitudes or orientations of energy—Extraversion (E) or Introversion (I). (In MBTI 'Extraversion' is spelt with an 'a'.) The next two are opposite mental functions—how we go about gathering information about the world, our perception—Sensing (S) or Intuition (N) and how we reach conclusions about what we have perceived, our judgment—Thinking (T) or Feeling (F). Myers added a fourth pair of opposite attitudes, reflecting our orientation towards the world—Judging (J) or Perceiving (P).

Both Jung and Myers assumed that people are born with a preference for one of each pair of these opposing tendencies. Therefore, within the MBTI model, with all possible combinations, you get sixteen different personality types.

The first paired preferences—Extraversion (E) and Introversion (I) are about energy flow and focus. If you are an extravert you tend to focus on and be energised by the outer world of people and things. You will therefore tend to become de-energised and tired if you spend too much time by yourself. In contrast, if you are an introvert you tend to focus on and be energised by your inner world of thoughts and reflections. If you are with people for too long you will become de-energised and tired. Remember, with all the pairs we are not talking about either/or, we are talking about *preference* so you will be drawn towards both, but to one more than the other.

The next preference is about how you take in information and perceive the world. Do you rely primarily on your five senses as a means of gathering information and prefer things presented to you in an exact and sequential manner? If so, you have a preference for Sensing (S) and you are very aware of your physical surroundings. Or do you gather information using your five senses then immediately translate it through your intuition, looking for possibilities, meanings and the relationships between and among variables? If so, you prefer Intuition (N) and have a preference for looking beyond what is actually there. For example, two friends are walking in a garden—one preferring Sensing, the other Intuition. The sensor will notice the different trees, birds and flowers and also be able to name many of them. The intuitive will, through association with what she perceives, have a flow of thoughts and feelings that will often take her mind elsewhere. Which do you think you are?

The third preference is about how you go about making decisions. Do you prefer to make logical decisions—in which case you have a preference for Thinking (T), or do you prefer to make decisions based on what is important to you and/or to others and have a preference for Feeling (F)? Remember, I am only talking about decision-making style here. Although Thinking and Feeling are different processes they often result in the same outcome.

For example, a couple are re-evaluating a decision about their son taking a family car one Saturday night. The car was promised to him earlier in the week to go to a party. The second family car has had to go to the garage for repairs unexpectedly. The parents' final decision is that they will drive him to the party and then go on to their party.

The Thinking mother believes it is important for their son to learn that in life 'things don't always turn out as planned', and although he will be angry with their decision they should be responsible parents. The Feeling father wonders, 'How would I feel if suddenly I was told I couldn't have the car when I had been promised it?' He decides he would feel angry. He also remembers that when he was young one of the ways his parents demonstrated their love for him was to show him that life does not always go as expected. He decides that although their son will be angry it is important to stick to their re-evaluated decision.

The difference between the two processes is that the Thinking mother is objective and removed while the Feeling father is totally involved in a subjective evaluation. Both care, think and feel, but the routes by which each arrives at the final conclusion are very different.

The final preference is to do with how we like to structure our outer world. This is the one I can usually tell by looking at a person's desk or bedroom floor. A person who prefers judging (J) likes a structured, well-organised, decisive lifestyle. Their desk will tend to be neat, especially at the end of the day. At night when they take off their clothes they will tend to put them neatly on a chair or hang them up. A perceiver (P) prefers a less decisive lifestyle that goes with the flow. Their desk will usually have piles of documents on it. They usually know where things are and they will only clean it up when they are having difficulty locating things. When they take their clothes off they might just step out of them and leave them where they fall or throw them onto a chair. They will perhaps sort them out for the wash or hang them up after several days when they feel things have got out of hand.

To assist you in working out which are your natural preferences I have included a table listing likely characteristics for each preference. You might like to refer to it now (see page 126).

PERSONALITY TYPE AND MIDLIFE TRANSITION

If on reading the table you are feeling confused, it could be because you are at midlife. When we are moving through midlife transition an interesting thing happens. The primary task of the first half of life is for us to develop a firm sense of identity by adapting ourself to the world we grow up in. Ideally this development occurs primarily through putting energy into our natural gifts, the psychological type preferences we are born with. If this has occurred throughout our childhood and teenage development, in our twenties and thirties we will have dependable and preferred ways of remaining energised (E or I), taking in information (N or S), arriving at decisions (T or F) and structuring our world (P or J). If all goes well we will have a well-developed personality and identity which provide a confident base for us to make good decisions about career and relationships.

As mentioned earlier, type theory says that we have all the type preferences available to us. We use each of them to function effectively, and we do develop some skills in our non-preferred areas. However, during the first half of life most of our energy is put into development of our preferred way of being. Many of the behaviours and attitudes associated with the non-preferred areas are, for the most part, ignored and pushed out of consciousness into our personal unconscious. However, around midlife, as we increasingly get in touch with our unconscious, we start being drawn to our non-preferences.

EMERGENCE OF NON-PREFERENCES AT MIDLIFE

Knowing our own personality type can help us to understand some of our atypical feelings and thoughts at midlife. At midlife as we hear the inner voices from our non-preferred functions

Table of MBTI preferences

Listed below are characteristics often found in people with that particular preference.

Where do you prefer to focus your attention? From where do you get energy?

Extraversion (E)	Introversion (I)
Focus on the external environment	Focus on the inner world
Prefer to communicate through talking	Prefer to communicate through writing
Talk things over in order to understand	Think things through to understand
Learn best by discussing or doing	Learn best through reflection
Broad range of interests	Few interests, but in depth
Sociable and expressive	Private and contained
Readily take initiative	Take initiative with the very important

How do you prefer to deal with information?

Sensing (S)	Intuition (N)
Drawn to present realities	Drawn to future possibilities
Focus on what is real and actual	Focus on patterns and meaning
Move methodically towards conclusions	Form quick conclusions—follow hunches
Understand through application	Understand by clarifying ideas, theories
Remember details with ease	Remember details as part of pattern
Trust experience	Trust inspiration
Factual	Imaginative

How might others describe you when you make decisions?

Thinking (T)	Feeling (F)
Analytical	Empathetic
Use logic to make decisions	Use personal values to make decisions
Strive for objective truth	Strive for harmony
May be 'tough-minded'	May be 'tender hearted'
Use cause-and-effect thinking	Guided by personal values
Reasonable	Compassionate
Fair—want people treated equally	Fair—want people treated as individuals

How do you prefer to deal with the outer world?

Judging (J)	Perceiving (P)
Organised, systematic, structured	Flexible, spontaneous, casual
Decisive	Like to leave things open to change
Make short- and long-term plans	Adapt and change plans with ease
Avoid last-minute rush	Energised by last-minute rush

Note: Some words used for the MBTI preferences are familiar to us, but their meaning is somewhat different to our everyday use. 'Extravert' does not mean talkative; 'Introvert' does not mean shy; 'Feeling' does not mean emotional; 'Judging' does not mean judgmental; and 'Perceiving' does not mean perceptive.

and attitudes and start using them, life can seem disorientating. This is because the non-preferred functions and attitudes are at an immature level compared to the development of our preferred functions and attitudes. When we first use them, life can seem a combination of exciting, bewildering, challenging, surprising and tiring all at the one time. From observing myself, clients and friends I have gained some understanding of how the non-preferred functions and attitudes emerge at midlife.

A person who prefers Extraversion (E) in the first half of life will find at midlife they are wanting increasingly to seek out more time to be alone. I remember feeling slightly 'at sea' when I first spent days by myself. Now I love having days to myself. I thrive on having time to be with myself, my thoughts and feelings. I find my energy levels decrease if I don't create this solitude. In contrast, a friend with a preference for Introversion (I) has expressed surprise as she feels more drawn to being in the outer world at midlife, and finds she is even energised by it.

For a woman who prefers Sensing (S), development of Intuition (N) at midlife means she has a desire to pay attention to new possibilities in life, to act on hunches and to see patterns not noticed before. She finds she is interested in things she has previously thought were irrelevant or tedious. In contrast to her main focus in the first half of life, she is now interested in abstract things that have no immediate practical value. She can be attracted to the arts. She may want to visit art galleries, appreciate sculpture, write poetry or learn about psychology. In contrast to earlier times, she will also start paying attention to her hunches, and be guided by them without having to research them first by gathering the facts.

A woman, like myself, who has preferred Intuition (N), finds midlife Sensing (S) involves being much more in the present than she has ever been before. At midlife I have spent long periods of time in the botanical gardens or on my own front verandah just looking, smelling, listening and at times touching the beautiful trees, flowers and birds around me. When I take my golden retriever, Bertie, for a walk I literally stop to smell the roses. As I sit in my bedroom to read over what I have written, I appreciate the comfort of the armchair I sit on, the beauty of the room, the colour of the leaves on the gum trees outside my bedroom widow. I notice so much more of what is around me. I also enjoy raking up the autumn leaves in my garden. And I have started growing tomatoes in the summer. I might have done some of these things before, but that was because they needed to be done. Now I want to do them because of my pure enjoyment of them.

A Thinking (T) woman finds midlife Feeling (F) involves discovering her softer side. She notices she is now emotionally touched by expressions of feeling which she would barely have noticed before midlife. She may be having a cup of coffee with a friend and will become tearful when the friend recounts an emotional moment in her week. Or strong emotions are felt and tears come when others express care or they hear a 'soppy' song. One friend of mine now cries every time she hears 'Waltzing Matilda'. If you are in this group you can feel somewhat overwhelmed and out of control of your feelings at this stage of life.

A Feeling (F) woman finds midlife Thinking (T) involves a push to be more separate from others, to focus on her own needs. At first she can feel guilty about doing things for herself, although once she sees the personal benefits at midlife she enjoys her more self-centred world. She also has a desire to be more assertive and gain a greater sense of her own personal power and will start challenging authority for the first time. She begins to realise she can have an impact on her world, take more control of her life and discovers she can use her thinking to move her life in a new direction. A Feeling friend of mine has recently gained a greater sense of competence, control and self-esteem by very successfully dealing with the sale of her home, and buying of a new home. Something she had thought she needed others to help her with she was able to do herself. With encouragement she recognised she had effective thinking and that there was nothing others could do that she couldn't.

For a woman who has preferred a Judging (J) attitude to life, midlife Perceiving (P) can be seen in a more relaxed approach to routine and structure. A client with a preference for Judging spent many years enjoying the routine and structure of primary school teaching and running a well-ordered home. She has now taken leave, and finds she is enjoying sleeping in then waking up to see what the day will bring, rather than feeling it should be planned. She is also less interested in planning the future. For a woman who has a preference for Perceiving (P), there might not be such a significant change. This is because life has con-tinually pushed her into her Judging (J) attitude whether she likes it or not. At school when young, at work and in running a home, women are continually pushed into a structured, orderly lifestyle. So for a woman who has a preference for Perceiving, such as myself, I find as I have become clearer about my self I have created a lifestyle which is structured, although in a relaxed, flexible way. Others looking on may be surprised that I am achieving anything, as my work and my living of life are so intertwined. It is planned, but very much in my own idio-syncratic way. This suits me perfectly.

And so if we move through midlife transition and listen to our inner voice, we begin to mellow, to become more rounded. We never become as easily adept at our non-preferences as we are with our preferences; however, we will engage more completely in life and our Self as we learn to enjoy all ways of being.

Part 3
Creating your new personal world

Finding our true Self will only lead to frustration, and even depression, if we can't create a personal world where we can be our Self. This is the midlife task women find most difficult. We struggle with creating a personal world where we can honour our Self.

14

Are you a 'human being' or a 'human doing'?

Work like you don't need the money.
Love like you've never been hurt.
Dance like nobody is watching.

Mark Twain

Few of us grew up in an environment where we were encouraged to 'be' ourselves. Mum said, 'Be a good girl and help me with your baby brother', our teacher said, 'Sit up straight and look to the front and don't talk', Dad said, 'Stiff upper lip', and all expressed pleasure in us if we achieved a school report with lots of 'A's. We learnt from an early age that we were acceptable, which we interpreted as lovable, if we put on a mask and acted or did things that our parents and significant others wanted of us.

As adults we have continued this pattern in an effort to make us feel good about ourselves. We say to ourselves, 'I will be more lovable, more valuable, if I just get that promotion, or I keep the house perfectly tidy or I hold the best party!' If we achieve a goal we may feel more satisfied with ourself but in the long term all this 'doing' will make no difference. For love is not something won through doing, but is rather a spontaneous expression of affection and warmth towards one's own or another's being. What we don't realise is that if we give up our true Self to be busy doing things that have little meaning for us, empty feelings are inevitable as in the process we have already rejected our Self.

Why is it so difficult to step out of this 'doing' cycle? Perhaps we have a fear that if we are just ourself nobody will like us. This fear can start from when young when we wanted to please those whom we were dependent upon, such as parents and teachers. This fear forced us to mask our true feelings and to go along with all that was expected of us. This mask hid the real Self not just from others, but also from ourself. We hid those parts of ourself that were unacceptable, too frightening or too painful to be confronted. For example, women often have the mask of a smiling face even when feeling very sad inside. They will often also keep themselves busy 'doing' to distract themselves from their sadness and fear. And the more they smile and the busier they become the more they delude themselves that life is fine. They continue to believe doing is living and their life is measured by what is accomplished.

All this busyness and role playing takes a lot of energy. By the time we reach midlife many of us get tired. Our psyche and our body says 'Enough!' Unfortunately, the masks and roles we have taken on have become so much part of our being that we don't realise they are not the real us. We have become so identified with them that we cannot conceive the possibility of being otherwise.

In the Western world we live in a society where we tend to overvalue masculine qualities and undervalue the feminine ones. This type of world makes it very difficult for us to move into a life of greater balance. These two words, masculine and feminine, are so highly charged that before I continue I will explain what I mean by them. To do this I will introduce you to Jess.

Jess, aged 42, is experiencing inner conflict. Work is important and there is much to be done, with deadlines to be met. Increasingly there is little time left to be with family and friends or to just have time to 'smell the roses'.

As you read this brief description did you think Jess was male or female? The description could be of either. The point is that all of us, both men and women, have masculine and feminine energies within us. Jess is feeling the conflict between the psychological masculine energy of doing and the psychological feminine energy of being. In Western culture these two terms, feminine and masculine, have for so long been identified with gender it makes it difficult for us to view them in another way. However, it is this psychological view of masculinity and femininity that I want to explore here. It is a focus on a psychic rather than a biological difference.

Jung was the first psychologist to say that all human beings were made up of both masculine and feminine energies. According to Jung, although women might equate themselves with just the feminine, and men with just the masculine, we are in fact all androgynous. If we are biologically female our ego, our persona, what we show to the outside world, is feminine. To balance this in our psyche we carry inside ourselves our own inner masculinity, what Jung called the animus. It is the reverse in a man and he carries within himself his own inner femininity, the anima.

If this is so, what makes men and women different? Could it be that as a woman identifies consciously with her ego, her persona and her femininity, her masculine side is unconscious to her? And that a man does the opposite? There have been many articles and books written discussing whether the apparent differences between men and women are due to underlying biological or psychological dissimilarities or due to socially assigned roles and conditioning. That is not something I wish to pursue here. The area I do wish to explore is how we can make use of these masculine and feminine psychic energies to create a personal world where we create balance for ourselves between 'being' and 'doing'.

The ancient Chinese book of wisdom, the *I Ching*, also recognises these two polarities. It says that in all of us there is the Yang, the creative masculine and the Yin, the receptive feminine. The Yang energy within us makes us goal orientated and disciplines us to make the most of our gifts. In contrast, Yin energy makes us experience our 'being'. It has its own rhythms, slower than those of the masculine and moving in a meandering and often circular motion, helping us find what is meaningful to us. This feminine energy may work hard but it still remains focused on living life in a way that reflects 'being'.

Within each individual's psyche there is a continual attempt to balance these two energies. With growing maturity, especially once having moved into midlife transition, we have an inner push from our psyche to avoid the extreme of either polarity. Hopefully, through noticing our Self and our life, we gradually find a refined balance between being and doing. At midlife we can best meet our psychological, emotional, intellectual and physical needs by aiming for this middle path between feminine and masculine, between feeling and thinking, between unconscious and conscious, between inner journey and outer journey, between being and doing.

Most people of the generation now at midlife in Western society, both women and men, have not identified with a strong feminine energy. Many of our families and schools related more to the masculine energy and were dominated by masculine values. Our world was geared to order, to goal orientated ideals, and to success in life through 'doing'. Dr Benjamin Spock's best-selling book on baby and child care was a big influence on many of our parents when we were young. It was predominantly based on masculine values of structure, timetabling and routine. Many of our parents dared not allow themselves to react spontaneously to our unexpected demands. Any of our feelings and thoughts that were not in accordance with what they thought acceptable were often rejected. Within this attitude there was no room for either us or our parents to relax into our 'being'. Geared to doing things efficiently, many parents wouldn't allow their own life or the life of their children to just happen. With incomplete access to their own feminine energy many of our parents could not pass on to us a joy in living, a belief in just being and a trust in life. Consequently we grew up with a feeling of our 'being' not being good enough; instead we attempted to justify our very existence by keeping busy by 'doing'.

With the impact of the feminist movement many women of our generation are competing in the masculine, animus, Yang-dominated business world. They have shown that they can achieve in this way; however, it is often at the expense of the honouring of their feminine energy. Many women are now refusing to be caught up in this world. Many are leaving their corporate jobs to start their own businesses. They often do this around midlife. Women increasingly find organisations domi-nated by masculine, Yang energy impossible to work in if they want to create a personal world where they have a balance between 'being' and 'doing'. As they discover that balancing their male and female energies in their professional life leads to greater work satisfaction and effectiveness, they are attracted to 'doing it their way'.

As we move in to midlife we all have to find our own way of creating a balance between being and doing, between feeling and thinking, between a spontaneous and a planned life. A combination of these qualities of the feminine and the masculine energies allows us to become completely natural yet completely appropriate in our actions. My personal experience has shown me that there is a lot of trial and error involved in achieving this, and that it requires an ongoing vigilance to balance these polarities.

In his book *Fear Of Life*, Dr Alexander Lowen makes certain distinctions between 'being' and 'doing'. As you will see from the following personal examples, I have found these distinctions useful in moving my life in a more balanced direction. As you read through them, think about how you could relate them to your work, your recreation and free time. Is there something you could do straight away to move towards greater balance in your life?

DISTINCTION NUMBER ONE—GOAL FOCUSED VERSUS PROCESS FOCUSED

'Doing' involves the conscious application of our energies to a task. Our ego sets a goal and then controls our actions to achieve it. On the other hand, an activity where we have little or no ego involvement belongs to the realm of being. Therefore, if the goal is secondary to the action, the activity qualifies as 'being' more than 'doing'. For example, as I walk my dog, Bertie, I often stroll through the local wetlands with my senses enveloped in the sights and scents around me. I am in a state of being. When I walk briskly through the same area with the goal of giving my body aerobic exercise I am in a state of doing. All productive activities such as preparing a meal, folding the washing or writing a book can be aspects of doing, however if we are more focused on being present in the process than in achieving the goal, these activities become an aspect of being. Similarly, dancing is an activity usually in the mode of being, except if we are trying to learn some complicated new dance step or impress somebody, in which case it could become more about doing.

DISTINCTION NUMBER TWO—OUTER VERSUS INNER

This distinction concerns the focus of our activity. When the focus is mainly on our outer world it is a doing activity. When the focus is mainly on our inner, feeling world it is an activity of being. A personal example might help here. Like most women with a family I spend a lot of time folding washing. I have rarely found this activity irksome, although it is still a repetitive task that has to be done. A couple of years ago I consciously decided to try something new. While folding the washing I thought of the person whose washing I was folding. It was usually either one of my children or me. I suddenly found that folding washing took on a completely different role in my day. It was like a meditation. At times it took much longer as I dwelt on all the loving, tender feelings I had for that person. And sometimes that person was me! So being occurs when our focus is more on our inner feelings.

In contrast, doing involves an outer focus. For example, if I am folding my washing in a hurry in order to pack in time to catch a plane, my actions are dominated by the goal and my feelings are irrelevant. In fact my feelings of anxiety may handicap me reaching my goal so I will usually block them and so transform myself into a form of robot until the goal is achieved.

In a similar vein, as I am writing this book I am aware of the need to balance the outer orientated goal of writing a book with the inner journey and the feelings evoked as I write. Throughout the early stages of the writing my main focus has been on my feelings of joy, connectedness and pleasure as I write. Towards the end there has been more of a focus on the goal of completing the book. Keeping a balance between the two is vital to me as I create a feeling of balance around my writing.

DISTINCTION NUMBER THREE—PUSH VERSUS FLOW

When an activity flows it is an aspect of being. When it has the quality of push, it belongs to doing. When an activity flows for us we experience pleasure because it stems directly from a desire within ourself and leads to the satisfaction of that need. An activity in which push is required is painful because it is against our desire and so requires a conscious effort through the use of will. For example, if as I sit here in front of my computer my writing connects me to feelings and thoughts inside myself I wish to express, my writing time flows as I do it in a sense of being rather than doing. However, if I have to write a professional report that holds no intrinsic interest for me it feels like more of a push. It is work. In this doing mode I am often much less effective.

We can apply the same distinction of flow and push to playing sport and any recreational activity. If our main focus is to push towards a goal or winning, the activity is no longer pleasure and recreation, but work. In the same way if we are doing work where we are absorbed in the experience it is no longer work but play.

A similar distinction can be used when considering our experience of sex. If we are absorbed in the experience and go with the flow, we remain in a state of being. The overall experience overrides the goal of orgasm. If, however, we are too focused on the final goal, we remain in a state of doing, and are not able to fully engage our being in the experience.

During midlife transition, as I have gradually become more of a human being than a human doing I have found that I have much more energy for pleasure and creativity in my new personal world. I move more easily from being to doing and then back again as I experience my day. And the more I practise, the more flexible I become about how I can spend my time. I no longer have fixed ideas or habits determining how I live. With growing confidence, I experience the excitement of new ways of doing and being as I live my life. And as I continue to bring these two energies within me into harmony I realise how unique each of our individual lifestyles can be.

15

Remaining distracted from your Self through your addictions

An addict attempts to fill a terrible emptiness inside.
But it's spiritual emptiness, not a physical emptiness.

Marion Woodman, *Conscious Femininity*

The most obvious way we keep ourselves busy and distracted from our Self is through our addictions. I am not necessarily only talking here about chemical addiction, but rather a broader definition of 'avoidance of Self' by any repetitive, harmful activity. Most of us have addictions of this type in various forms and degrees. This might be anything from exercising extensively, obsessively doing work, including housework, always caring for others or getting 'hooked' on chat lines on the internet. We may be a compulsive gambler, a compulsive spender or a compulsive hoarder. There are also the more obvious chemical addictions of substance abuse including alcohol, marijuana, heroin and cocaine; or the misuse of legal pharmaceutical drugs, such as antidepressants, sedatives and painkillers. Many of us are also addicted to one or more of nicotine, caffeine, chocolate or to overeating in general.

Most of us are not even aware of our addictions. Many addictions are encouraged in our society. Serious addictions create a barrier between our conscious world and our unconscious world. We unconsciously create such barriers to distract us from the painful feelings and thoughts that dwell just below the surface of our consciousness; the feelings and thoughts we don't want to confront. If we want to become more complete in our Self at midlife we have to confront this pain.

In the Western world we have created an addictive society. As we have become obsessed with materialism we have robbed ourselves of a society with soul. For a great number of people the experience of everyday life is one of loneliness, alienation, emptiness and meaninglessness. Many use addictions as a way of numbing themselves from this pain in their life and it takes determination and personal commitment to break out of the addictive cycle. It is especially difficult when we are caught up in an addictive system—whether this is in our family, our place of work, the friends we mix with or the community we live in. From my observation, we often have to step out of the addictive system in order to heal and rid ourselves of our personal addictions.

Addictions that are seen as acceptable, even worthy by our society are particularly insidious. In the woman's world the acceptable, even rewarded addiction is caring for others. Girls of my generation were often made to feel like second-class citizens. In many families boys were naturally given more attention, just because they were boys. At home the girls helped Mum care for the 'men of the family'. Even when it might not have been their natural inclination, they carved out an identity as nurturer. Self-esteem came from an ability to relate to and anticipate others' needs. Young girls and women learnt to feel good about themselves by being indispensable. Often this tendency went way beyond normal nurturing.

Many women still believe they are not of value just as they are. They frequently over-serve and over-care in their relationships in the hope that it will make them feel better. This attitude is a trap, and often leads to overprotective or obsessive relationships with husbands, partners, children, grandchildren, friends and community. At midlife women can end up in a round of frantic activity in an attempt to attain an identity through doing. I am not saying here that any person who shows a caring attitude and actions for another should stop it. This of course wouldn't make sense. We all want to be able to show care and love to our family, friends and others. The difference between genuine caring and 'unhealthy' caring can be found in the motivation behind the behaviour.

CASE STUDY—ROSEMARY

Rosemary, aged 44, presented with a typical story of female addiction. A student counsellor, divorced and with two teenage children, she came to see me to tell me her story. Recently she collapsed at work. She has high blood pressure and heart fibulations. Her doctor has put her on medication. She also told her she has to make some lifestyle changes and referred her to me for counselling.

Rosemary grew up in a large country town. She has two brothers and a sister. She is the second eldest, with an older brother. Her father was a hardworking general practitioner. Her mother had been a nurse before marrying, and had done clerical work for her husband in the medical practice as the children got older. Rosemary had been a good student. She went to the city where she completed an Arts degree, with teaching in mind. Halfway through she combined it with a Social Work degree. On completing her course she worked as a secondary school teacher, and a couple of evenings a week also worked for a voluntary counselling service. She stopped paid work while the children were young, although she continued with the voluntary counselling, except when they were babies. Once the youngest child went to school ten years ago, she took a position as a part-time counsellor at a private school. On divorcing three years ago she took this on full time. This is the work she is doing now. She says she has always thrown herself into her job. She prides herself on always being available for emergencies, even after hours.

Ever since the birth of her first child she had a series of minor, and then not so minor illnesses. She ignored these, controlling the symptoms by taking medication. In the last couple of years she has experienced significant gynaecological problems. These she has not been able to ignore.

Rosemary's two children are excelling at school. She is very proud of this and has always emphasised to them the importance of doing their best. Her eldest, a daughter, has recently been diagnosed with anorexia. This has been a very difficult time for Rosemary. She had not realised the severity of the problem. She feels guilty and wonders how she could have missed it. After several sessions Rosemary started to talk to me about her drinking. Heavy drinking has been a pattern for her since university. Her mother was also a heavy drinker. As I further explored Rosemary's family life as a child, it became evident that her mother, although hardworking, had little time for her. In fact, both parents were hardworking, but emotionally 'not there' for her or her siblings.

Rosemary has now decided to apply for long service leave for three months. At the moment we are exploring the idea of her attending an Alcoholics Anonymous support group. She has taken the big step of acknowledging her dependence and given herself the space to heal.

Rosemary's story is a typical story of a woman addict. First, in her family of origin there was a denial of her emotional world. Both parents were emotionally absent to her and there was no other significant adult giving her emotional support. As she was the eldest girl, her mother often looked to her for help with her siblings' care. Second, she chose a traditional woman's 'caring' profession where demands are great and salary is relatively poor. Third, she refused to pay attention to physical symptoms, except when they became severe. Fourth, she has projected her perfectionist tendencies onto her children. And finally, she has the tendency to increase the pressure in her life, while at the same time being oblivious to the effect on her and those around her.

When we give up an addiction we have to be careful not to substitute it with another. A former alcoholic who becomes an exercise fanatic has changed the content of her addiction, but the process stays the same. Some people may view obsessively exercising as a positive addiction. First of all, the phrase 'positive' addiction is a contradiction in terms. There is no such thing as an addiction that is beneficial. The very nature of addiction is that it takes you away from your Self and ultimately may kill you. And even if it doesn't kill you, an addiction robs you of feeling alive. It robs you of your life.

So if you wish to get to know your Self better, I suggest you observe yourself and assess what behaviours you may have unconsciously put into your life to take you away from your Self. If you are game, you might even like to ask a trusted friend or partner for their honest assessment.

16

Meaningful simplicity

Simplification of outward life is not enough. But I am starting with the outside. I am looking at the outside of a shell, the outside of my life— the shell. The complete answer is not to be found on the outside, in an outward mode of living. This is only a technique, a road to grace. The final answer, I know, is always inside. But the outside can give a clue, can help one to find the inside answer. One is free, like the hermit crab, to change one's shell.

Anne Morrow Lindbergh, *Gift from the Sea*

Several years ago my life was like a tangled ball of wool. I would look at it and feel overwhelmed, and want to throw it back into the sewing basket and forget about it. I did not know where to start unravelling. However, once I pushed myself to take the small step of untangling an accessible thread, other threads appeared. Each step I took made it freer and easier to work with.

By midlife we've often been so busy being the good partner, the good career woman, the good mother, the good daughter, the good daughter-in-law, the good sister, the good friend, the good employee we have created a complex, tangled lifestyle. For a variety of reasons we have lost sight of what we want to be and do. Without meaning to, we have allowed others to control our life. No wonder it feels complicated and full of stress as we move this way and that trying to keep everybody happy. From my experience and observation, this is a sure way of eventually pleasing nobody, including ourself.

Perhaps as young girls we weren't encouraged to make our own decisions. We might have easygoing, compliant personalities and find decision-making stressful and so developed the habit of allowing others to make decisions for us. Or we hadn't realised that it was reasonable to express and live out our own dreams. Either way, we have gone along with what other people have wanted to do, or wanted us to do, for so long that we have lost sight of what is important to us.

If you've spent years not knowing what you really want of your life, it can seem an onerous step to slow down and take time out and figure it out. It often seems easier to keep on doing things that we don't want to do. Our lives get frittered away. And the things that we know in our hearts we want, get put aside. We yearn for a simpler, more meaningful life as we navigate our way through our daily activities and responsibilities. Clients say to me, 'How can I possibly simplify my life? I've got my work, my partner, my kids, my mortgage and car repayments, and my ageing parents to think about. There's no space for me to take the time to stop and simplify.'

Torn between these pressures it feels as if there's no way we could add one more thing, like simplifying, to our list of things to do. Yet if we don't take this time out to simplify at midlife we get to desperation point.

Meaningful simplicity is not about getting rid of everything we've worked hard for. It's about deciding what's most important to us, and gradually letting go of the things that aren't.

It's about making wise decisions about how we live our life from now on. Trying to do it all has meant we have developed a lifestyle so full that it takes all our effort to manage it. And often we are managing things we don't even want to. Once we put into place the principles of meaningful simplicity we start to live the life we want to live. In the process we also nurture our Self.

What may signify a simple life to you may be very different to what signifies a simple life for someone else. Simplicity is a relative concept. It is also a very personal one. When a person is wishing for a simpler life they are yearning for a life that has more personal meaning. For example, at the moment I am writing this book. I get up early, I write, I read, I visit the library, I speak to publishers and editors. I am also spending time with my three teenage children and running a business. I make time for friends, family, exercise and hobbies. Because my life revolves around my priorities and my values, much of the time my life flows along and feels simple. Another person who has different values and priorities to me might find my life anything but simple.

When you are thinking of bringing meaningful simplicity into your life you need to spend some time pondering what this means for you personally. Start by asking yourself some key questions. No one knows the pattern of your days or what is in your heart better than you do; and no one knows your answers to these questions better than you do.

SIX KEY QUESTIONS TO BRING MEANINGFUL SIMPLICITY INTO YOUR LIFE

1 What are my top four or five priorities in life? (Chapter 6 on making your values conscious should assist you.)

2 If I simplify my life using these priorities as a guide, what will it look like? What will it feel like?
3 What will I gain by making my life simpler?
4 What do I need to remove from my life to simplify it?
5 Once I have simplified my life, how can I ensure it does not become complicated again?
6 Can I make some easy changes right now or do I have to make some significant changes first?

CREATE PERSONAL SPACE

Do whatever you need to do to create the personal space to focus on these questions. Remove distractions so you can listen carefully for the answers. You may be able to find some reflective time at home or work. However, most of us need to get right away from our everyday environment to feel free of distractions. Creating this reflective time was a major turning point in my life.

We can feel uncomfortable when we sit still and pay attention to our inner voice. We hear things we don't want to hear. We may be told that we need to change our job, our career or many of our relationships. Often we have kept our life complicated and busy so that we don't have time to hear these inner messages.

OUR FANTASIES ARE A GUIDE

Our fantasies can be a strong guide for us at this time of simplifying. We may fantasise about living out in the countryside. Or we may fantasise about moving into a one-bedroom flat. In his book *Understanding the Midlife Crisis*, Peter O'Connor suggests that we can best serve ourselves by looking at our fantasies for their inner meaning and then attempt a change within our present situation in the light of this inner meaning. For example, if you have a fantasy to live out in the countryside you could ask yourself what it is about this fantasy that is attractive to you and incorporate these attributes into your present lifestyle. If the answer is that you have a yearning to spend more time outside in touch with nature, further ask yourself how you can create this time for yourself now. Perhaps you could go for walks in the local parks and gardens, feeling the grass under your feet and watching the birds and other wildlife. Or you could plan to spend some weekends renting a cottage in the countryside. If you fantasise about escaping to a one-bedroom flat your questioning might lead you to accept that you feel overburdened by your family responsibilities. Can you shed some of them and create more time for yourself by being more assertive with your family about sharing the family workload?

So 'meaningful simplicity' is not necessarily about literally following our fantasies and moving to 'a cabin in the woods'. This is a big leap. Many people have left everything behind only to find that it's not necessarily simpler or what suits them. Tempting as it might be at times, acting on our fantasies and escaping our present complicated life is not the only way to create a simple life. It's also not a realistic option for most of us. Instead, fantasies can be used symbolically to light our way to a simpler, more meaningful life.

SMALL CHANGES START THE SIMPLIFYING PROCESS

To start the process of simplifying you can make easy changes that create a difference. For example, you can free up small pockets of time to exercise, to spend time in nature, to be in solitude and for keeping a journal. These small changes create physical and mental space where answers to our questions come more easily.

By making some simple changes straight away you free up time to figure out what really matters to you. Focus on your top four or five priorities. Use these as a guide. Start arranging your days so that as much as possible they revolve around these priorities. You won't be able to rid yourself of all complications, especially at first. But you can start eliminating the clutter by shedding those things that no longer add value to your life. By removing these, you create space for yourself, your thoughts, your feelings and those things that truly matter to you. You learn to be selective. That's a big part of what meaningful simplicity is about.

EFFECTIVE, SIGNIFICANT CHANGE TAKES TIME

How quickly we make changes will depend to some extent on where our life is at the moment as well as on the type of person we are. Some people thrive on change and once they have decided to simplify will move along quickly. Others are more cautious around change and will want to move slowly. However, if you are leading the full life that in our society is considered a normal life, you can't realistically expect to simplify it in one week. Effective change takes time. It took many years to build up your tangled life and it can take some time to effectively simplify it. I found that once I began to be selective in my day-to-day life in order to free up time, an amazing thing happened. Each step I took made it easier to take the next step. As I freed up a little bit of time, other ways started occurring to me. The effect was exponential.

DISCOVER SIMPLE WAYS TO NURTURE YOURSELF

When I ask clients how they nurture themselves they often have no idea what I mean. They have never realised it is something they should do. As you free up time, discover simple ways to nurture yourself. At first you might find this difficult. Perhaps you haven't nurtured yourself before. It may take several years of exploration to find what truly nurtures your soul. Listen to music, run a bath, burn your favourite incense and oils, sit in the sunshine. Finding simple ways daily to nurture yourself puts you in a more open, relaxed state of mind. This open-mindedness will help you in the simplifying process.

WE HAVE TO SHED AS WE SHIFT

Some people think that simplifying our life is about cleaning out our wardrobe and kitchen cupboards. Certainly it can assist to get rid of lots of physical clutter in our lives. However, as you throw out those old utensils and clothes, also throw out all the beliefs and attitudes that no longer serve you.

As you focus on what is most important, you will realise that there are many aspects of your life that are no longer meaningful to you. For many women, family and friendship demands, and demanding work or community involvement are the major complications of their lives. We do want to honour many of our family responsibilities and many of us need to earn a living. If you've got a demanding, time-consuming job, that alone might be sufficient reason to shed some other responsibilities.

Perhaps you have a job or a significant relationship that does not seem to be working for you. It is demanding too much of your time, too much of your energy, and therefore too much of your life. However, while living a complicated life it can seem impossible to work out how to make effective significant change. If the thought of doing so has your mind reeling, don't tackle the big issues yet. Instead, look at the rest of your life and see what you can remove from it. By opening up some space for relaxing times you will open up your mind to possibilities you have never thought of.

PRUNING BACK

We know that if our garden is to thrive we need to 'prune back' some of the old, dead wood to make room for the new growth. In a similar way, at midlife we need to 'prune back' some of our old ways of life that no longer serve us, to make way for new ways of being. Clients often express bewilderment at this feeling of wanting to 'prune back'. They are aware that there are many aspects of their life that have no meaning for them anymore. They feel guilt as they no longer want to spend those evenings at book club, dining with old school friends or supporting their local community group. They feel guilt at the thought of saying 'no'. It seems a huge step to say 'no' to these activities, to free up time to walk the dog, or to potter in the garden, or to do that special course, or to spend time with family and close friends, or to just spend time alone. Yet this is what we have to do if we are to create space for a more personally meaningful life.

So when wanting to simplify our life significantly we at first clear it of many people and activities that no longer have the same meaning for us. It sounds harsh but to me it is almost inevitable when at midlife transition. At this stage life can often be lonely. If you are not used to this feeling, it can at first feel terrifying. There is temptation to fall into old patterns and to once again say 'yes' to people and activities we know no longer fulfil us, just to fill up these lonely times. However, depending on how quickly you want to turn your life around, I believe it is important to put up with the loneliness. Eventually this feeling goes away as we discover and start making friends with new parts of ourselves while in solitude.

IS THIS THE RIGHT DECISION FOR ME?

Many of us are so caught up in pleasing others, we automatically agree to others' invitations or suggestions even when we know deep down that we don't want to. In order to stop doing this we need to find a way to turn off our automatic pilot button and turn on our thinking button. At this time in my own life I found an effective strategy was to continually ask myself, 'Is this the right decision for me?' whenever I was asked or was deciding to do something. Even now, several years later I continue to find this strategy useful when making decisions.

I have also found it important to check that I am not making an ego-driven decision. That is, am I choosing to do something because it will make me look good in another's or my own eyes or am I choosing in a way that fits in with my key priorities? If I become ego-driven I can easily start complicating my lifestyle again by saying 'yes' to work, social and leisure activities that lack personal meaning.

LET GO OF WANTING TO PLEASE

When we want to simplify we have to let go of our desire to please others. As much as possible be honest in your responses, while at the same time being sensitive. To say to a friend, 'I won't be coming to tennis anymore. I have enjoyed playing, however I have decided to cut back on my activities and tennis is one of the things I am choosing not to do anymore', is part of being assertive. If the person does not accept, or does not seem to hear what you are saying, use the 'broken record technique' of continuing to repeat your message. Assertiveness and the 'broken record technique' are explained in the next chapter. Eventually the person will get the message even if they are not happy with your decision. This is something I have learnt to live with. For if I want to please my Self by developing a personally meaningful life, I assume I won't always be able to please others.

Over the course of several years of putting into place many of the above strategies I have gradually made many changes and have developed a lifestyle that much of the time ideally suits me. For me, simplifying my life has meant that I choose to run a business from home. I start my day with time to write, contemplate, walk my dog, talk with my children, telephone clients, listen to some of my favourite radio programs and, when there is time, chat on the phone to close friends. My working life and my personal life are interwoven. This works well for me. As I make personal and professional decisions during my day, my key priorities and values guide me.

I have found that by simplifying, by slowing down, by breaking some of my consuming and spending habits, and by adopting simple pleasures for myself, my friends and my family, I have created a mostly joyous and fulfilling life. I also don't feel as though I am working as hard to maintain it.

17

Asserting your Self to create your world

Ex-pression is the opposite of de-pression.
Whenever we de-press, we usually need to ex-press.

Sark, *Living Juicy*

The alarm clock rings. Amanda rolls over and bangs the black, plastic button down thinking to herself, 'Oh, I feel so tired. Why do I always wake up feeling so tired these days? What's wrong with me?' She slowly gets out of bed to start her day. After showering and dressing, she gathers up the dirty washing from around the bedroom and carries it downstairs.

Her daughter, Emma, is in the kitchen having breakfast. She asks Amanda if she has seen her sports uniform. Amanda fetches it from the bottom of Emma's laundry pile. She hands it to her, saying in a terse voice, 'If you'd taken your washing upstairs as I'd asked, you would have known where it was.'

It's now 7.45. Amanda wonders to herself, 'Is Ben up yet?' She listens. She can't hear the shower in the children's bathroom. She drags herself back upstairs. He is flat on his back sound asleep. The alarm clock lies on the floor. She thinks, 'Did he set it before he went to sleep? Did he turn it off? When will I be able to rely on him to get himself out of bed? I can't stand it. I feel like screaming.' She quickly calculates he has 35 minutes to shower, pack his bag, and eat breakfast if he is to catch the train to get to school on time. She thinks, 'I don't want anymore phone calls from his teacher asking me to try and make sure he gets there on time.' She stands at his door and in a tightly controlled voice says, 'Get up, Ben, you'll be late again. Get up.' He rolls over and says, 'Oh, Mum I've got plenty of time. Why do you have to be such a nag?' Halfway down the stairs she yells back, 'Just get up!'

Her husband, Ian, is now also in the kitchen, whistling as he gets ready to leave for work. Just before walking out the door he mentions that he bumped in to an old school friend and has asked him for dinner that evening. He pecks her goodbye on the cheek and says, 'Don't worry, you can keep it simple.' She reluctantly agrees, hoping he'll notice her lack of enthusiasm. He and Emma leave. After racing around tidying up and hanging out the washing, Amanda drives Ben to school on her way to work. It is a little out of her way but at least she knows he will get there on time.

Amanda arrives at work, sits down at her desk and realises she has a morning headache coming on. She takes an aspirin and starts to check a report. An hour later, when finished, she goes downstairs to the coffee shop and orders a coffee and a muffin. She's not hungry. She just feels like it. She also has a smoke in the breezeway before going back upstairs. A colleague comes up with another copy of the same report she has just corrected, saying, 'I have made some further changes. I hope it's not too much trouble. Can you check it again?' She hesitates, then says, 'Yes, that's fine.'

She starts to read but is having difficulty because of tears in her eyes. A friend comes up and says, 'Hi! How are you?'

Amanda puts her head in her hands and starts to weep quietly. 'What's the matter?' asks her friend. After a moment, Amanda responds, 'I don't know. It's lots of little things but not enough to cry over. I just feel so drained all the time. I don't know what's wrong with me.'

In my mid-thirties, when I first became a consultant to organisations, one of my first assignments was to design and run an assertiveness course. As I read books on assertiveness I was shocked to realise that I wasn't assertive in much of my own life. I read that we all have rights to express our thoughts, feelings and needs. Although we can't make others accept them, we always have a right to express them. Why hadn't I known this before? I also read about the communication skills needed to be assertive. In some situations I did use them. However, this was more by luck than conscious application.

Growing up in the 1950s and 1960s, I rarely saw assertiveness skills modelled. My world at home and school was authoritarian. I did what others told me to do. Luckily my parents were fairly liberal and so I wasn't too restricted in my home life. However, rarely was there room for disagreement and discussion. School was worse. There, none of the teachers seemed interested in our opinions.

After running that first course, and subsequent others, I have realised that most people are unskilled in assertiveness. Over the past ten years I have taught many women and men assertiveness skills in courses and individual counselling sessions. And I now believe it is the most important interpersonal skill if we are to create for ourselves a satisfying, meaningful personal world while at the same time maintaining satisfying relationships. To explain what I have learnt about assertiveness I will tell you about the work I did with Amanda.

AMANDA

At our first session, Amanda explained:

> I feel as though I've spent most of my life focusing on other people. I always want everything to be peaceful and harmonious, yet much of the time these days I feel as though there is a war raging inside me. I've got tired of trying to please everyone. I want to do something for myself. I'm not even sure what that is. I'd love some peace and quiet and some control over my life. I'd also like to get rid of these headaches, not feel so tired, and lose about 5 kilograms. Sometimes I do finally work out what I want, however, by the time I do, it's either too late to say anything or I'm so frustrated and angry I don't dare open my mouth in fear that I'll explode. Usually I do end up exploding at the children. And then I hate myself and feel so guilty. I always seem to be carrying around in my head all these thoughts of what I could have said, or should have said, but I never say anything. I'm hopeless. I would love to be able to know how I feel at the time and then be able to express it.

I explained to Amanda that if we do take the time to think about the circumstances we can usually identify what is causing our feelings. Such as: Ben doesn't get himself up; dinner guests are invited without consultation. Once we recognise the problem, we can then determine what we want, think of the different ways to achieve this, and then decide how to assert ourselves in order to accomplish it. Other times if we know something is worrying us but can't identify what the problem is, we can watch our body or behaviour for clues—such as anxiety, anger, feeling low or physical symptoms such as headaches. When any of these are happening we can stop and look around at our life and ask, *'What's bothering me?'*

Signs of the need for assertiveness are teeth-grinding, nail-biting, finger- or foot-tapping or jiggling, artificial nervous laughter, insomnia, churning stomach, tightening jaw, headaches, tight neck muscles and any other personal ways to express tension. Behaviours that may signal the need for assertiveness are lashing out, procrastination and feeling low.

Towards the end of the second session I suggested to Amanda that she keep a journal for the next week to help her become more aware of the connections between what was happening in her personal world, how she was feeling and thinking, and how it affected her body. After she had done this, I asked Amanda to decide on three areas to work on. She decided she wanted to first make changes around her home life. She wanted to:

1 have two evenings a week where she did not have to cook;
2 create time to pursue her interest in ceramics; and
3 have a time each week with her husband where they went out, just the two of them, for any or all of a meal, film, coffee and talk.

She also wanted to tackle the 'Ben waking up and getting to school' situation but decided she needed more time to think about it.

Amanda knew she needed to develop her assertive behaviour with her children and her husband if she was to start working towards achieving these three goals She had modelled her behaviour with her family from her own mother. She had been doing this for years and to break old patterns was not going to be easy. She also knew that once she started being assertive at home, she could then use the same skills to be assertive at work. I discussed several aspects of assertiveness with her:

- Assertive behaviour is about being able to express our own feelings, thoughts and wishes while at the same time respecting the right of others to do the same. Assertive people can also express their personal likes and interests spontaneously; talk about themselves without being self-conscious; accept compliments comfortably; disagree with someone openly; view mistakes positively and learn from them; and say 'no'.

- To come across assertively it is important to be clear about what our rights in the situation are. Often we have 'unconstructive self-talk' that sabotages our efforts to be assertive. The next chapter looks at ways to ensure that your self-talk is constructive.

- Being assertive doesn't necessarily mean that we get our wishes met. An aggressive person is more likely to get their needs met, however this is often at the expense of their relationships. A passive person rarely gets their needs met because they never make them known.

- Even if we do not get what we want, when we are assertive we behave in a way that ensures we do not continually come away from situations feeling bad about ourselves. We feel more confident and have the satisfaction that we did not let ourselves down, nor did we abuse the rights of others. We show respect for ourselves, while at the same time maintaining respect for others. We become more relaxed in interpersonal situations, and as a result we are more fun to be with.

- When we are first assertive with a person we have not been assertive with before, they are often shocked. Our behaviour may be perceived as aggressiveness if in the past we have been passive in a similar situation. Gradually, the person will get used to our new behaviour and respect us more for it.
- We often need to use the 'broken record technique'—that is, we need to say the same assertive statement several times before it is actually heard. It feels a bit strange at first, however it does work.

I asked Amanda to choose one of her situations for us to role-play together. I suggested she choose the easiest situation first as I wanted her to give herself the greatest chance of being successful. She could then rehearse by closing her eyes and visualising the situation and imagining the words to use. As well as asking her to think carefully about the words she used, I emphasised that it was important for her to focus on appropriate body language and tone of voice. To assist, I suggested she follow three steps in her assertive statement:

Step 1   Show you understand the other person's perspective.

Step 2   Say how you are feeling or thinking.

Step 3   Say what you want to happen.

Amanda's assertive statement to the family

Amanda decided that at a family meal when her two children and her husband were together at the weekend she would say:

- I realise you all have busy lives too

however

- I do not want to be cooking the evening meal every night any longer

- and so I would like the three of you to think about how you might be able to create two of the evening meals each week.

I suggested to Amanda that she use 'however', rather than 'but', between the first two statements, as 'but' made them sound more confrontational.

This was the start of a dialogue within the family around the work and responsibility of providing meals. I reminded Amanda about the broken record technique where she repeated the three steps to assertiveness, creating different dialogue where necessary, when she wanted to get her feelings, thoughts and ideas across. Over time Amanda was able to use these steps to tackle a variety of aspects of her personal and work life. Often, just before being assertive she became very tense. This was to be expected as it was a very new behaviour in that situation for her. The stress would decrease over time. I taught her a simple deep breathing relaxation technique which she used just before speaking.

Over the next six months Amanda gradually was able to make many of the changes she wanted. As I had warned her, many people were shocked by her new behaviour and did not respond favourably at first. However, eventually many of her requests were met. She had created space to pursue some of her own interests. Her headaches decreased and she was feeling an increased energy for her life.

Since first running the course on assertiveness twelve years ago I have decided that assertiveness is the most important interpersonal skill for developing self-confidence, self-esteem and effective, intimate relationships. If we are passive we end up with a whole lot of feelings burning up inside us, creating tension and ultimately physical and psychological ill health.

If we are aggressive, we get our feelings out but wonder why we do not have comfortable relationships with people.

Developing my assertiveness skills was also the key for me to begin directing my own life and shaping it to be more congruent with the person I am.

18

Your thoughts create your world

My new world is a reflection of my new thinking.
It is a joy and a delight to plant new seeds,
for I know these seeds will become my new experiences.
All is well in my world.

Louise L. Hay, *You Can Heal Your Life*

If being assertive is merely the direct and appropriate expression of our thoughts, feelings and needs, why is it so difficult for us? In reality, even when we know and practise the skills involved, many of us are afraid of being as assertive as we would like to be. We are afraid of speaking openly and honestly about what we think, feel and need and then acting on our desires because we have so many self-limiting beliefs.

In the past, parents, other significant adults and society often had certain expectations of young girls. They were expected to please. They were expected to think of others. They were expected to not be demanding. They were expected to be passive. They were not meant to value their skills. Although now society's expectations have changed quite considerably, many of these messages are still echoing deep inside us and they can still shape our world. Often, we still want to please;

we still think of others' needs before our own; we are quiet; we are passive; we don't assert our skills; we don't assert ourselves.

We are constantly creating internal dialogue about ourself and what is happening in our life. Mostly we express it subvocally in our thoughts. Sometimes we express it out loud. No matter what the circumstances, it is quite normal for the mind to process constantly what it is observing. And the things we focus on most are ourself and the world we choose to observe.

For many people, especially those prone to addiction, this internal chatter tends to be extreme bursts of negative thinking. This continual negative chatter leads to low self-esteem, acts as a negative filter to what is happening in life, and inevitably leads to feelings of powerlessness about being able to positively direct one's life.

Our thinking is effective when it enables us to feel good about ourselves and to behave towards others in ways that work well for them and for us. Effective thinking helps us to create a personal world that honours the person we are. We commonly think that outer events or situations are directly responsible for our subsequent feelings and behaviour. However, how we respond to a situation will be a result of how we interpret it. And how we interpret it will depend on our inner thinking and self-talk. For example, if you say to yourself, '*I can't stand upsetting others*' or '*I can't stand people being angry with me*', your thinking encourages you to avoid outer disharmony and conflict. This avoidance stops you from speaking openly and honestly. That is, it stops you from asserting yourself. You temporarily avoid upset feelings, however, this is at the expense of you being true to yourself. Your thinking ultimately leads to inner disharmony and conflict, a poor sense of Self and an unfulfilling personal world.

Our beliefs, thoughts and attitudes are the vital link between an event and the subsequent feelings and responses we have to it. While many of our thinking habits are accurate and useful, producing appropriate behavioural and emotional responses, some are self-limiting and counterproductive. They can cause us to respond in a way that limits us in being able to assert ourselves and take control of and create the life we want.

If you want to create a personal world to suit your Self, you need to identify, challenge and replace any self-limiting thoughts. This requires a deliberate effort. Thoughts are often outside your awareness and so you need to stop and listen to your thoughts to determine if they are self-limiting. Once you learn to notice them, you are able to replace them with more productive thoughts where necessary. This is an important step for all of us at midlife.

I do not mean for you to develop positive thinking at the expense of truth of feeling. For example, I would not want you to replace '*I can't stand people being angry with me*' with '*I don't mind it when people are angry with me*'. This would be denying your true feelings. Rather, I am suggesting you take a more reasonable, rational view of life—thinking more accurately and realistically. For example, '*I don't like it when people are angry with me. However, I can stand it, it won't kill me and I need to be able to put up with people being upset with me if I am to start saying what I want and directing my life.*' It is up to you to use your own words and to work out what sounds right for you. Altering our thought patterns naturally takes time and practice.

THREE KEY STEPS TO CHALLENGE YOUR THINKING

1 Stop and listen to what is going on in your head, so you can identify what you are thinking and saying to yourself.

2 Determine whether your thoughts are self-limiting and counterproductive and lead to negative and unhelpful feelings and behaviours.

3 If they are, substitute them with other thoughts that you know will work better for you.

I have found several self-limiting thoughts most responsible for non-assertive behaviour. It helps to become familiar with these categories so you can recognise them whenever they appear. As you read through them, think of times when a similar thought pattern has stopped you acting assertively in your life. In your own words, create a substitute thought pattern to assist you in becoming more assertive.

One of the most common self-limiting thoughts is: *'If I am assertive others will get angry with me and that will be devastating.'* A more reasonable, self-constructive thought is: *'If I am assertive I do not know what the result will be. They might feel closer to me, respect me more, appreciate what I say, or get angry. No matter what the response, I will feel better in the long run for having spoken up. If the person is angry with me, I can handle it. I won't like it, however it won't devastate me.'*

Several years ago a friend of mine quoted to me a saying of his that was so powerful for me at the time that I put it up on my kitchen wall of sayings. It is still there today and I often read it to remind myself of its wisdom.

'If you suppress your emotions to spare others' feelings, you suffer the pain.'

So, another common self-limiting belief is: *'When I am assertive I may hurt the other person's feelings and I will be responsible for their pain.'* A more reasonable, self-constructive thought is: *'When I am assertive I may hurt the other person's feelings, however I can say other things to show them that I care about them while also being direct about what I think, feel or need. Most people are not as fragile as I imagine. If I have expressed myself appropriately I can reassure myself that I am responsible for my feelings and they are responsible for theirs.'*

One of the most important assertive responses is to be able to say 'no'—and to be able to say it without feeling guilty. If you have the self-limiting belief, *'It is wrong and selfish to turn down an invitation or a request. People won't like me if I do'* you will be continually allowing others to determine how you spend your precious time. A much more constructive belief is: *'It is OK to consider my needs before others. I can't please others all the time if I want to create a personal world that suits my Self.'*

Another powerful self-limiting belief that will stop you being assertive is: *'Assertive women are cold, hard-hearted and selfish. People will view me this way if I am assertive.'* Some unaware individuals might want you to believe this, to stop you from asserting yourself, however my experience has led me to believe: *'Assertive women are direct and honest. They show respect for other people's thoughts, feelings and needs while they also show respect for their own. Assertive women have healthy relationships.'*

At times, self-limiting thoughts have stopped me being open and honest about what I thought, felt or needed. Gradually I have learnt to observe my thoughts, and challenge and change them where necessary. Sometimes it might take me hours or days to work through these three steps. Other times I am able to do it on the spot.

There are other self-limiting thoughts that decrease our motivation to find out more about our Self and create a new personal world. As you read through them, assess whether any of these self-limiting thoughts are stopping you from moving your life forward.

If you say to yourself, '*I need to be able to do everything well*', you might decide not to try something new in the fear that you won't live up to your expectations. Often people say to me, 'I would love to write, or paint, or sculpt', but they seem fearful of taking a first, small step towards their goal. I believe it is often a self-limiting belief of needing to do well that stops many of us even trying a new skill. Instead we can develop the constructive belief: '*I will give it a try. I have nothing to lose. I'll focus on the enjoyment of the experience, rather than the outcome, knowing I am learning something new about myself and my world. If I do it well that will be an added bonus.*'

Another self-limiting belief is where we think in extremes. For example, taking a couple of occurrences and blowing them up into a general rule about ourself. I hear women saying, '*I'm always incompetent with money matters.*' On questioning I will often find that it is just that they have got used to others handling 'money matters' for them. If they think carefully they can always come up with examples of where they have been competent with money. A more self-constructive belief is: '*Sometimes I feel incompetent with money matters. Other times I have managed money well. I can learn what I need to about managing my finances. Then I will feel competent.*'

A common self-limiting belief is when we 'make mountains out of mole-hills'. We experience everyday mishaps as catastrophes. In doing this we unnessarily magnify things—especially our emotions. We use such words as: '*I can't stand it, it is awful, it is terrible.*' We can substitute this thinking with: '*I don't like it. I would prefer it was different. However, I can stand it, I will keep it in perspective and I will deal with it the best I can.*'

A final, most destructive self-limiting belief is when you label yourself. For example, you take an isolated situation such as not being able to assert yourself and use this as a blanket statement to describe yourself as a whole; for example: *'I am a wimp.'* The result of this is that you tend to perceive yourself as you believe yourself to be. It is difficult to create new perceptions about yourself and your world if you carry a label around about yourself. Ask yourself: 'If I wore a T-shirt with the word "wimp" written on it, how would I feel and behave with that label on me? Could this be similar to me carrying around a label on the inside of me? Do I put labels on myself and others?' A self-constructive way of dealing with this situation is to describe the specific situation instead of using the all-encompassing label. It is better to say: *'I didn't assert myself that time, however I will reflect on it, and learn from it and plan to do better next time'*, rather than, *'I am a wimp'*. Remember, what you do is different from who you are.

If you reflect on some of the difficult situations in your life, you may realise that unproductive thinking has been adding to your stress. It limits your ability to find effective and creative solutions to the myriad of difficult situations you will inevitably face as you pass through midlife transition. Your thinking is something you can learn to challenge. Make sure it is working well for you and assisting you as much as possible to create a satisfying personal world.

I suggest you now look at three areas of your life where you want to make changes. Become aware of any self-limiting thought patterns around these situations and decide from today to challenge them. Write self-constructive thought patterns on a card if necessary and carry them around with you to remind you. You will be surprised at how much your world starts to change once you start challenging your thinking. For remember:

YOUR THOUGHTS CREATE YOUR WORLD

19

Changing Self—changing relationships

The integration of our shadow requires that we live responsibly in
society but also more honestly with ourselves and in our relationships.

James Hollis, *The Middle Passage: From Misery to Meaning in Midlife*

Nothing has a stronger influence psychologically on their environment
and especially on their children than the unlived life of the parent.

C. G. Jung

As we find more of our Self at midlife we change, and
inevitably our relationships change. As discussed earlier,
when we are young we bury inside ourselves personal attributes
that we perceive as unacceptable by the significant people
around us. Some of these buried selves we project onto our environment. As we move through midlife transition and gather in
these projections, our perception of our Self and our world,
including the people in it, will change. The relationships most
affected are those with long-term partners, children, parents,
siblings and friends. Our perception of and relationship to our
work also changes.

OUR CHANGING RELATIONSHIP WITH A LONG-TERM PARTNER

When we partner at a young age, we tend to partner with somebody on whom we have projected disowned parts of our Self. Rather than develop these attributes in our Self, we 'marry' them. This is an oversimplification; however, for women of the 'baby boomer' generation it is probably closer to the truth than not. In our twenties, despite often having qualifications and our own jobs, many of us were still heavily influenced by the role expectation placed on women. Although in many ways empowered to live our own life and achieve our own desires, we still succumbed to the model set by our mother, encouraged by our father, and reinforced by society. While often still pursuing a working life outside the home, we constructed our marital home in a sex stereotypical way and fell into a traditional woman's role with our partner.

As we move into midlife transition this way of being a couple is challenged and destabilised as each partner starts wanting to develop parts of themselves that were originally buried or projected onto the other. Women often become aware of this unsettled feeling earlier than do men. One of the reasons for this is that women are typically more aware of what is going on inside themselves. Through our friendships we share and explore our emotional world more than do men. Through our female friendships we surround ourselves with our own unofficial counsellors.

Typically, a woman starts feeling unsettled around 35 years of age. The pressure often does not come to a head until her early forties. This unsettled feeling comes from her psyche, which is sending her messages to become conscious of those parts of her Self that are buried in her unconscious, or projected onto others. This is what she has to do to move towards individuation; to move towards balance and wholeness.

We usually project more onto our long-term partner than onto anybody else. We particularly project the contra-sexual element—the animus—on to our 'man'. In Jungian terms, our animus is our experience of the masculine, influenced by our father, our culture, and other factors unique to us. Our animus gives us a sense of our capacities and abilities, and helps us focus our energies to achieve what we want for ourselves in the outer world. Many of us, despite our own qualifications and work experience, projected our animus onto our man when we partnered. This projection can also occur in homosexual relationships where one may take on the more masculine role, while the other the feminine. I am not saying that this projection would have been as strong as it was for our mothers, however it was often still there. Through this projection and also because of societal expectations, he was perceived as the partner who would most use his capacities and abilities to achieve in the outer world. During midlife transition we are pulled by our psyche to take back our animus projection. As we do this, we start perceiving our partner and his role in our life differently. We also start seeing our Self, and the way we want to live, differently.

Similarly, our partner fell in love with us when he projected onto us aspects of himself, including his anima. His anima represents his internalised experience of the feminine, influenced by his mother and other women, and also coloured by something unique to him. His experience of his anima represents his relationship to his own body, his feeling and instinctive life, and his capacity for relationships with others. Through projection of his anima he saw us as the one to take care of these aspects of his life. Similar to the work we have to do, he has to take back his projection of the feminine, and take it within himself in order to move towards individuation. To make these changes while in a long-term relationship, with all the habitual patterns of relating that go with it, is not easy. We will no longer be his 'princess'. In the same way he will no longer be our 'knight in shining armour'.

For much of history, marriage served as a vehicle for the maintenance and transmission of values, traditions and power. Traditionally marriage was based on a hierarchical structure where the husband was seen as dominant and superior to his wife. Her inferiority was reinforced by lack of education and work experience, which also made her financially dependent. Our generation has been caught between two worlds. Many of us were brought up with a very traditional understanding of how a couple should be. Most of our parents acted out very traditional gender specific roles all their lives. Many of our mothers had limited, if any, qualifications. Few pursued careers or had financial independence. Many in our generation obtained qualifications and had a career and at the same time created marriages using the sex stereotypical paradigm for marriage that our parents used. Since the 1970s there has been a deluge of information to assist us in our growing self-awareness, as well as heighten our expectations about what we want from an intimate relationship. The women's movement has opened up our awareness to greater possibilities for our-selves and our lives, way beyond anything our mother's generation thought possible for women.

Marriage is such a commitment that I now marvel at how so many of us managed to take such a step at an age when the majority of us were still so unaware. Any intimate relationship can only be as good as the relationship we have with ourselves. How well we know ourselves not only determines the type of people we are attracted to, but also the quality of our relationships—and the quality of our relationships also depends on how effectively we relate to each other.

We partnered at a time when there was little information to help us develop self-awareness or the skills to manage relationships effectively. As we have felt the inner push for self-development at midlife, we have found there now is ready access to this information. There is also easy access to adult courses to train or retrain if necessary. Women no longer see themselves as necessarily financially dependent on the man in their life.

Caught between the world of our mothers and the world we are now in, we have set ourselves on a collision course. We may have acted out the traditional role of our mothers and have built up certain expectations in our family. At midlife we develop personally and realise we wish to develop a different role within the family context.

It is often much more difficult for us women to affirm our own needs within the family context because of the enormous claims that are made on us by relationships within the family. Our feminine consciousness makes us very aware of our surroundings and of the needs of others. At midlife it is very difficult to put our own needs ahead of those we love.

Some argue that personal development is narcissistic. It is not, as long as we are determined to fulfil our own potential while at the same time granting the same right to others, especially our partner and children. Balancing our obligations to others and the obligation to ourself is admittedly difficult, but it is important to at least try. It is the ideal that each person in a relationship has the support of the other to make the most of themself. However, if a couple have had years together relating in a more traditional way, they may not have the communication skills, the 'goodwill' or energy to create a new way of working together to allow this to happen.

By midlife, many marriages or long-term relationships are over or in trouble. In the past, couples who lived through the withdrawal of projections were under too much societal and economic pressure to find alternatives. Counselling was also rarely seen as a viable option. Inability to deal with the real issues often led to affairs, alcohol and drug abuse, over-attachment to work and children, or habitual illness and depression. Positive choices were generally beyond a person's reach.

Today women and men do have choices. Many couples at midlife attend individual and couple's counselling. There is also a proliferation of books and courses to assist people to develop essential relationship skills. Many find they are able to grow both individually and together to develop a new, more open and equal relationship. And painful as the choice to separate may be, it is also a viable option today. For many it is not as bad as remaining within a structure which seems like a slow death of Self.

We have become so dominated by the idea of 'falling in love' that we can still hold onto this paradigm and search for it after separation or divorce while moving through transition. So many of our songs and movies reinforce our expectations that when we meet the right one, the earth will move and we will feel a fluttering in our heart. But 'falling in love' involves projecting aspects of oneself onto another person. Once we start moving through midlife transition and start feeling more complete in ourselves, this outcome becomes less possible.

Many of us change our views only after a lot of trial and error when we discover for ourselves that falling in love is not always the best basis for an enduring relationship. For many, this trial and error exploration of what comprises an effective relationship occurs after separation and divorce.

The model that many of us based our intimate relationships on in the first half of life is one of 'coupledom'. After becoming more complete in our Self through midlife transition no longer are we looking to the other person to make us feel whole. An alternative relationship model for the second half of life is one where each person is primarily in charge of his or her own journey of Self-understanding and of developing their own fulfilling personal life. Through their intimate relationships, individuals support and encourage each other, but they cannot perform tasks of development or individuation for the other.

Ideally an intimate relationship in the second half of life offers companionship, mutual respect, support, encouragement, nurturing, sexual expression, some shared interests and compassion. Another essential ingredient is open, honest communication. For if one is not prepared to truly engage in ongoing dialogue about the difficult issues as well as the good times, then one is not prepared to put in what is required for long-term intimacy.

CHANGING RELATIONSHIPS WITH OUR CHILDREN
Recently a friend overheard this conversation between a mother and her son.

Mother: How did your tennis go?
Son: I lost.
Mother: What do you mean, you lost? What went wrong?

Son: He was pretty good. I also hit quite a few out.

Mother: That shouldn't happen—you should win at that level.
            You can do better than that.

Son: I'm sorry, it just happened. Can I go out with some
            friends this afternoon?

Mother: No. You certainly won't. You can go down to the hit-
            up wall and practise until you don't hit any out.

I believe that most, if not all parents who put excessive pressure on their children to succeed are living out their own 'unlived' selves through them. This particularly may be true in the case of those women who have not been encouraged to develop and make use of their talents and don't feel empowered in the world. A parent usually projects most strongly onto the same-sex child. However, this is not the case with the projection of the anima or animus, which is usually projected on to the opposite-sex child. Many sons have had to carry their mother's ambitions, while many daughters carry their father's feeling side.

If they are to move towards individuation at midlife many women do need to withdraw projections from their children and allow them the space to pursue their own ambitions. I am not suggesting parents shouldn't have aspirations for their children. It is healthy to encourage them in their endeavours. However, it is important for all parents to be focused on living their own lives, thus allowing their children to do the same. And as parents let their children go during midlife, they help themselves as well as their children, as they release energy for their own ongoing development.

Due to the social changes in the past 30 years, mainly through the achievements of the women's movement, a large group of women have spent the first half of life attaining competence in the outer world, usually through the development of a career. For these women the animus is very well developed. A significant task for them at midlife may be to develop their anima. For these women midlife may involve more anima-like issues, such as conflict over whether or not to have a baby.

At midlife the greatest change for me in my relationship with my children has been that as I have found more of myself and then been willing to share many of these parts of myself with them, our relationship has become more relaxed, open, loving and fun.

CHANGING RELATIONSHIPS WITH SISTERS AND BROTHERS

While reading through the literature on relationship changes at midlife, nobody mentions the destabilising effect the midlife passage can have on our relationships with siblings. If we are living alongside a sister as we grow up, she is a sitting target for our shadow projections, as we are for hers. 'I am the more out-going one; she is the shy one. I am the messy one; she is the tidy one. I am the thoughtful one; she is the thoughtless one.' There is a myriad of extreme qualities that we disown or take on. As we move towards a more balanced view of ourselves, we realise we can both be thoughtful and thoughtless and so we take back our projections from each other. For those who have several sisters there is more than one 'sister hanger' from which to remove projections. A brother may also be a target for a sister's projections; however, this will be a projection of her animus. She may project onto him her own abilities and strengths in mastering the world.

My experience at midlife has been that as I have withdrawn projections from my siblings we have gradually learnt to relate more openly with each other. Concurrently, we have become more open in our communication generally and have gradually developed a depth and authenticity I have greatly valued during midlife transition. For example, my relationship with my sister has dramatically changed. We have always supported each other, however at a certain stage during midlife transition I said to her: *'I don't know why as yet but at the moment I need lots of space and so I won't be seeing as much of you for a while.'* I realise now that deep down I felt as though I couldn't find the real me with all the family labelling that could inevitably happen when I was with my sister or one of my brothers. If my parents had been alive I believe I would have had to keep them at a distance as well. I have noticed that clients who are going through personal transition express a similar need to have space from their siblings and parents. That is, to not see as much, if anything, of their 'family of origin' while they are trying to become clear about who they really are. Sorting out our relationships and our projections with our siblings plays an important role in our midlife transition.

CHANGING RELATIONSHIPS WITH FRIENDS

As we gather in projections and unbury parts of our Self, our friendship groups may change. As we develop new interests we will meet people who share a liking for the things we are increasingly valuing in our own life. Past friendships based on partner or children associations or past interests may not have the same pull as they did in the first half of life.

CHANGING RELATIONSHIPS WITH WORK

In the first half of life we work to establish ourselves in the world. This may be work for money in some form of outside employment, or it may be work in our home looking after children, a husband, a partner and others who may be dependent on us. Our main focus is on the extrinsic needs of ourself and others. We earn money to buy the things we need for ourself and our family. We perform tasks at home to ensure our children's and partner's needs are taken care of.

In the second half of life we are focused on intrinsic needs. It is the time in life when we ideally have a vocation. That is, we do work that fulfils needs which are deeply connected with our Self. There is seldom a straight path to a vocation, but rather lots of twists and turns that create personal experience enabling the unfolding of a vocation. Friends and family say to me as I spend many hours writing, 'You are working so hard', and I respond, 'But it's not work. I love it.' We still might do some other work to meet our financial needs; however, as much as possible, I believe we nurture our Self immensely if we find work about which we have some passion. This is why people will often have a 'career crisis' at midlife. As we start connecting with our Self, our work role from the first half of life loses its significance. We yearn for a vocation; a way of working which holds more personal meaning beyond the financial reward and status.

CHANGING RELATIONSHIPS WITH PARENTS

My parents aren't alive and so I am in a very different position to many others at midlife. When my father died suddenly ten years ago it was a turning point for me. I spent several months reassessing my world and my priorities. I believe it is a significant turning point for most of us when our final parent dies. Alongside the grief, there is the realisation that no longer are we anyone's daughter. No longer are those powerful, parental influences present, often encouraging a false sense of Self acquired during the first half of life.

Relationships with parents are complex. Whether or not our parents are still alive, an important task for all of us as we move through midlife is to differentiate our world from theirs. Did our parents feel empowered? Did they feel angry? Did they feel nurtured? Did they feel sad? As long as any of these remain unconscious to us we may continue to carry the unexpressed feelings and unlived lives of our parents.

Many of us spend much time unconsciously asking permission or 'checking in' with an invisible parent inside ourselves as to how we should live. Inner, self-limiting thoughts or dialogue can be a much greater influence in our day-to-day life than we ever imagine. If we ask ourselves, 'Who is this person I am consulting?' more than likely we will come up with the answer that it is our mother, father or a significant adult who is still talking to us from deep inside ourselves. We need to challenge this thinking. As we realise new parts of our Self we might want to express parts of our Self that they do not approve of, such as our artistic talent, our desire to reject the traditional female role or a need to be honest about our sexual preference.

As we examine the role of others in our lives we can at times feel very critical of them. Some even say that psychotherapy is all about blaming others for one's difficulties. My experience has been far from this. As I have become more accepting of my own vulnerability and 'human frailties' I have become more accepting of others.

20

Synchronicity is a guide to a new direction

Synchronistic events ... almost invariably accompany the crucial
phases of the process of individuation. But too often they pass unnoticed,
because the individual has not learned to watch for such coincidences.

C.G. Jung, *Man and his Symbols*

By definition one cannot cause synchronistic events, but on the basis
of observations in this area ... it does seem possible to develop in a
person an increased sensitivity to synchronistic events, and especially
a capacity to harmonize one's life with such occurrences.

Ira Progoff, *Jung, Synchronicity and Human Destiny*

Have you ever had the experience of thinking of an old friend you haven't thought of, seen or spoken to in a long time, when the phone rings and there she is asking how you are? Or perhaps at a time when you needed guidance you had an astrological or tarot reading, or dabbled in numerology. If so, you have been tapping in to what Jung coined 'synchronicity'.

I first noticed synchronicity in my life at the start of midlife. I was 35 years old and I had just learnt to meditate. I didn't know what synchronicity was. I did know, however, that there was something unusual happening in my life. I kept on having experiences that evoked in me a sense of awe and wonder. I experienced moments of truth and intuitive knowing. Looking back I can now see that as a result of this first awareness of synchronistic events with the ensuing feelings, I was led to an energy and passion for activities and to a potential I had never previously suspected. I felt there was a new purpose and meaning to my life. Since then I have often experienced what I now understand to be synchronicity. It hasn't always had such a profound impact on me as it did that first time I noticed it. However, I have found that at midlife it has been an invaluable guide in helping me to access untapped energy, passion and talents that connect me deeply with my Self.

The first time I noticed synchronicity in my life was when I went away on a holiday with a friend, Tess. The inspiration for the holiday came to me while meditating. It was a very unusual thing for me to do as I left three young children at home. I have described some of the events previously. I will recount these events plus other synchronous personal experiences to explain:

- Jung's explanation of synchronicity;
- why synchronicity is an important process to make use of at midlife;
- how we can open ourselves up to synchronicity; and
- how to encourage its presence in our life.

On the holiday, the events that happened were:

1 I went scuba diving for the first time. To do this I had overcome significant fear and anxiety. After the first day of diving I stood on the prow of the boat and leant into the wind thinking to myself, 'I can do anything if I just put my mind to it.'

2 At the holiday resort there were several businessmen who, I gradually realised, appreciated being able to talk over their work problems with me. Towards the end of the holiday while talking with one of them I had this fleeting thought, 'I would be as bright if not brighter than these men. I am just as articulate, if not more so. I also probably have more formal qualifications. Why is it that they are doing more interesting, challenging, well-paid work with much greater recognition?'

3 On the following morning while having breakfast Tess turned to me and said, 'I think you will do something special with your work one day.' I was nonplussed. Her comment came out of the blue. I had not mentioned any of my inner thoughts to her. I was barely aware of them myself.

4 I had a prophetic daydream while flying back home. I put headphones on, lay back, closed my eyes and relaxed into the music. Suddenly I had a vision of myself speaking in front of a large group of people. I was dressed in a black dress and a bright jacket. It was 'corporate' dress. I hadn't ever dressed that way. As soon as I came out of this day-dream I started planning a new professional life.

5 As soon as I got home from holiday I started being proactive in creating this professional life. However, one day I started to question inwardly whether it was possible to make the transition from the education sector to setting up my own business in the corporate sector. As I was walking down the street wondering about this, I bumped into a woman I had met several years beforehand at a course. I asked about her life and she told me that six months beforehand she had left her job as a psychologist in the education sector, had spent six months working in a local consultancy firm, and now

was working with one of the country's top consultancies. I had the answer. It was possible.

As you read the above account you might have been saying to yourself, 'So what!' However, I was very aware there was something new happening in my life. It felt as if I was being led down a path. All I had to do was ask a question, then look for the sign posts to check I had read the signs properly.

Jung first introduced the term synchronicity to a small group of followers in 1928 and spoke publicly about it a couple of years later. It wasn't until 1952, after many years of careful empirical research that he published a paper entitled 'An Acausal Connecting Principle'. This was the first time synchronicity had been given psychological meaning. The simplest definition that Jung gave synchronicity was 'a meaningful coincidence'. I want to explain carefully what Jung meant by this because there is often a misunderstanding about what he was saying.

When we say something is 'meaningful' we usually mean it has touched one of our core values or it has had a big impact on our lives. A meaningful event might have one or both of these attributes. Synchronistic events move us deeply because there is a simultaneous occurrence of a certain psychological state in us with one or more external events that are meaningfully connected.

In the above example, my internal, emotional state and inner questioning about my work was reflected in the chance occurrence in the outer world when Tess said out of the blue that she thought I would do something special in my work one day. Similarly, when I was walking along the street wondering whether it was possible to make my planned work transition, my emotional, questioning state was reflected in the external event of the chance meeting with an old acquaintance showing me it was possible. In both these cases my inner thoughts were meaningfully connected with outer events in my world.

The *Macquarie Concise Dictionary* definition of coincidence is 'a striking occurrence of two or more events at one time apparently by mere chance'. In both of the above examples it was a chance occurrence that these people said what they did at the time. If they had known previously about my inner questioning, it would not be a coincidence. And this coincidental nature along with its meaningfulness for us is what makes something synchronistic.

When I have had a synchronistic experience I have found certain characteristics present:

- A new understanding becomes conscious to me. For example, in relation to the previous example, I had only ever thought of working for another employer or working as a counsellor in private practice.
- I am stretched to perceive myself in a new and different way. After my experiences of scuba diving, talking to businessmen and having my prophetic daydream I started to assess myself as capable of more than I had previously imagined. My mind started opening up to possibilities I had never before considered possible.
- I notice further events that help reinforce the feeling that I am on the right track. Just as I was questioning if it was possible to make the transition, an acquaintance appeared to demonstrate to me it was possible.
- The experience has occurred at points of important transition or a turning point in my life.

A couple of months ago I had what I regard as an extraordinary synchronistic experience. When I tried to explain it to family and friends there was no way they could understand how powerful an experience it had been for me. I had borrowed a rare book from the Council of Adult Education library. It was overdue and I was wondering how I could possibly get a copy to buy for myself. It was a fairly old, rare book and I knew it would continue to be useful for me in my writing. Where I do my food shopping there is a small second-hand bookshop. At this time I had been feeling a bit discouraged with the progress of my writing and was looking for a sign that I was on the right track. In the couple of hours before I was to do my shopping I kept on having this vision of myself walking into the second-hand bookshop and picking up this rare book. Each time I had the vision, I thought to myself, 'Don't be silly. It couldn't possibly be there.' I went shopping. I went across to the local library to see if they had a copy. They were closed. Feeling a little silly, I thought, 'Oh well, I may as well try the second-hand bookshop.' I walked back across the road in to the shop and straight up to a table where there was a heap of books and immediately picked up the rare book. I let out a yelp. The owner looked around. I tried to explain to him what had happened but he just looked at me as if I was a little odd. I paid and left the shop with my book. I also left knowing I was on the right track!

Synchronistic events are coincidences that hold a subjective meaning for us and like all things subjective, what we find meaningful another person might very well find meaningless. This is one of the reasons why it is easy for others to scoff at, dismiss or make fun of us when we talk about synchronicity in our lives. Like the story just recounted, some synchronistic events have a strong 'Aha!' sense about them. In others it may not be until much later that the significance of what occurred becomes clear. This sort of synchronicity has much more of an 'Oh, now I understand' sense to it. In some cases the external event occurs first and the internal, subjective meaning follows. In others, the meaningful coincidence is between an internal image, such as a dream or vision, as with the above example, and a subsequent, external event. In all of these synchronistic events, however, the connecting principle between inner and outer is the meaning of the event for the person involved.

It's important to understand that Jung wasn't saying that one event was causing the other. To say that we are, as a culture, used to thinking in terms of cause and effect would be an understatement. Cause-and-effect thinking is such a fundamental part of our Western mindset that we are hardly aware of it. That is, until we are faced with a sequence of events, such as the above, that by their very nature illustrate a different way for events to be connected.

But if it is not a cause and effect process, how is it happening?

Jung said that an archetype is always involved in true synchronicity. He said we encounter an archetype in powerful dreams, visions or synchronistic occurrences. Archetypes are operating deep within our psyche, creating order and patterns, in a similar way to how instincts operate on the physical body. In synchronicity, an archetype filters inner and outer events in such a way that meaning dawns in our consciousness. Their patterning effect is always happening unconsciously and this is why it is only in retrospect that we can see these connections.

The archetype is not causing the events. Since synchronicity is acausal—that is, without a cause—then we shouldn't slip into cause-and-effect thinking just because this is what we are used to. Rather the archetype is acting like a mediator in imparting the meaning. To make them meaningful, situations seem to cluster around the archetype in such a way that an alert and sensitive person can recognise at least a piece of the wisdom linked to that archetype. And if it is the Self archetype that situations form around, we will come away from the experience with increased wisdom about our Self.

Why did I only start recognising synchronicity in my life when I did? Was it because I was at the age when midlife transition commences? Was it because I had just started meditating? Why are some people more aware of synchronicity than others? Why am I sometimes more aware of it at one time than I am at another?

Jung said that at any time of transition in a person's life, synchronicity occurs more often. At midlife, when individuation is such a powerful force, the Self archetype, our inner guide, is activated. I believe there are certain things we can do at midlife to encourage its activation, and to encourage our noticing of it. This will in turn mean we notice more synchronicity in our life.

OPENING UP TO SYNCHRONICITY AT MIDLIFE

I have found synchronicity to be a strong, positive guide in midlife. Assuming this is so, how can we make best use of it? We can't make synchronicity happen; however, we can discipline ourselves to be more open and responsive to it. We are more likely to notice and act on guidance from synchronistic events at midlife if we focus on certain key factors.

First, it makes sense that we will be more likely to notice meaningful inner and outer events if we have already made ourselves aware of what is meaningful to us. Therefore to make ourselves more open to synchronicity, an important step is to identify our core values. Chapter 6 discusses ways to get in touch with and clarify your values. Bringing these values to consciousness will assist you on your way to bringing more synchronicity into your life.

Another key factor is whether you are open to new ideas and willing to at least give them a go. When counselling I notice there are clients willing to consider new ways of looking at situations and then there are others who come seemingly looking for help but who aren't ready to be open to new ways of thinking. Think about your own life. If you had a problem of direction, would you try something new? Would you consider analysing your own dreams, using meditation practice or putting yourself more in the way of synchronicity as a way of finding possible answers?

Third, we can use methods such as astrological and tarot readings or numerology. The random arrangement of cards, numbers or dice is presumed to have a meaningful relationship to the questions we are asking. However, we always have to keep in mind that once again it is not ourselves nor the cards, numbers or dice that cause or manipulate any such coincidences.

Once we think we have recognised some meaningful synchronicity in our lives it is up to us to decide what we do with the insight that comes. It is important to maintain a balanced perspective. Along with opening up our minds to different possible ways of seeking guidance, we need to make use of our conscious, analytical skills. When we have noticed a synchronistic sign, had an insightful dream, received an informative psychic reading, or tapped into meditative wisdom, we still have free will. We can still use conscious judgment and have freedom of choice about how we apply the information. For whatever assistance we get, we always want to remain personally empowered.

Since first starting to meditate I have noticed a great deal of synchronicity in my life. I believe this could be because meditation assists the subconscious to filter events for meaning. Some of the synchronistic events have been:

- receiving a very strong impression or thought of a person just before they telephone me or walk through the door;
- opening books at just the right page when doing research;
- walking into a second-hand bookshop and immediately picking up a rare book I had been thinking about the hour before;
- when doubting myself noticing a sign that helps reassure me I am on the right track; and
- meeting just the right person by pure chance at just the right moment, at a time of great need, or at a time of unusual openness.

Have you noticed any of these happening in your life recently?

SUGGESTED STEPS FOR INCREASING SYNCHRONICITY IN YOUR LIFE

As well as meditation and being clear about my values, I have used several other strategies to increase my awareness of synchronicity in my life. You might find the following suggestions interesting to try.

To start with, for several days train yourself to pay careful attention to outer events and the inner world of your thoughts, feelings and desires. Look for coincidences. Watch for synchronistic connections between events which cannot be explained through the law of cause and effect. You can also start looking for possible interpretations. Remember that thoughts and outer events may be days apart. Write down the things you notice.

Next, hold in your mind a specific question and watch for synchronistic experiences that may relate to that question. For example, a possible question is: 'What talent can I develop which will help me be more fulfilled in life?' While you are focusing on this question, certain activities may assist you such as meditation, walking in nature, listening to classical music, exploring a library or bookshop, or browsing through magazines.

Finally, continue to use any of the activities you found useful, however now focus on a new question: 'What do I need to keep doing to become more my Self?'

If you put these into practice you might be surprised with the results!

SYNCHRONICITY HELPS US TO NOTICE THE STORYLINE OF OUR LIFE

A good story has an interesting and well-constructed plot. When we first start reading a story we can't see the plan of the plot but as it becomes clearer, events which at first seemed random and meaningless turn out to be quite important. As I look back on my life I can now see a well-constructed plot made up from synchronistic events that have had an impact on me at different times in my life. Some of these events seemed meaningless, although at the time I did notice and remember them. They had a certain energy around them and as in a good story these synchronistic events have often had a powerful effect on me. They have given me a different way of seeing myself, a broader perspective on my life, or a broader perspective on my world.

Once I started recognising synchronicity in my life I was also confronted with the fact that sometimes the stories I wanted to believe about myself are not necessarily the stories

I am actually living or, more importantly, that I am meant to live.

So as friends tell you about the synchronicity in their lives, pay attention to your own resistance to believing that such events can happen. And when next time you personally experience synchronicity I hope you notice it and look further to what has occurred. If you do, then, the notion which Jung proposed in his understanding of synchronicity has served its highest purpose; to help you see the meaning of the stories you are living each day.

Part 4
The journey never ends

What they gradually realise is that the essentials for
establishing a new life are the inner resources they had within
them before they started the journey, and those discovered
and developed during the journey. They also find strength
from others who are, or who have been, on a journey similar
to their own.

All of these continue to be needed to create their new life.

THE JOURNEY NEVER ENDS

21

Balancing your inner and outer journey

And I'm frightened. I'm frightened of life beyond the wall.

Shirley Valentine

Our inner journey is a journey towards wholeness. At midlife our psyche has an inborn, evolutionary urge to push us to grow, to become whole, to become our Self, to become more of the unique person we always had the potential to be. To do this we make an inner journey to our unconscious, find buried parts of our Self, and make these parts conscious. This is what Jung called individuation and this process continues right through our life.

The inner journey is an expression of the feminine side of our nature. To support ourself in this journey we develop daily practices such as creating time for reflection, meditation, yoga, journal writing, creative pursuits and dream analysis. These practices help us to be present to just our Self and our unconscious world. As we honour our feminine side we also enjoy walking in nature and listening to the birds, nurturing our body, listening to music, and showing affection to the people we love.

We access our inner feminine side when we allow ourselves to let go, to stop trying to control both people and situations in our life, and to trust in fate and the natural flow and rhythm of life. We learn to wait patiently, listening to our inner voice and to the wisdom that comes from our feminine feeling and intuition.

We each choose our own way to encourage and continue our inner journey. A couple of years ago I read *Cave in the Snow*, a book about an English woman, Tenzin Palmo, who spent twelve years in a cave, mostly meditating. I was so amazed by the story that I bought several copies and gave them away to friends as Christmas presents. I know people who have met her since and they say she has a very special presence. She has been described as an enlightened being.

My friends use a variety of ways of nurturing their inner journey. One spends a month each year at her holiday house at the coast by herself not talking to anyone. She plays the piano. She writes. She draws. She sleeps. Another goes to India for a month each summer and spends hours sitting with thousands of others in the vicinity of their 'teacher'. Other friends pray in Christian churches. Another is part of a Buddhist group that meets regularly for group meditation. Some have daily practices in their home of meditation, creative pursuits and yoga. What are you doing to nurture your ongoing inner journey? Do you have a regular practice to centre you on your Self?

In his book *She*, Robert Johnson points out:

> A truly modern person cannot go off to a convent or the Himalayas exclusively to search for spirituality; nor can she pour herself exclusively into her family, profession, and practicality. It is the prime task of a truly modern mind to endure both the spiritual and the practical as the framework for her life.

We all gain from finding time for our inner journey while at the same time dealing with our everyday lives. Although not always easy, there are clear benefits in focusing on, and balancing these two worlds. The synergy between our inner and outer journey enhances our life.

This particularly became obvious to me as I started writing this book. When I started, I assumed that my inner journey through writing would be enhanced if I went away by myself where I wasn't distracted by my everyday, outer life. However, once I started observing my writing process, I realised that some of my best work, some of my most profound insights about my Self and my inner world came as I was having to deal with the demands of my outer world. For example, early on in my writing I had a rare, and distressing argument with one of my children. Afterwards I could see that the upset arose because of my writing. I was not as available as I had been in the past. Just before the argument, I had said to my children, 'I won't be getting dinner tonight because I am too tired from writing.' I may as well have had a new lover standing beside me. My children sensed that there was a new entity in Mum's life. It was changing the way I behaved. It was changing my availability to them.

My inner writing journey meant my outer world was changing and people around me were noticing. That night I went to bed thinking, 'I'll just have to get away if I'm going to get some proper writing time.' The next morning I woke up and started writing with enormous energy and didn't stop for several hours. My inner writing journey had been stimulated by my outer journey. Gradually I realised I didn't have to separate the two. They were both an important part of my life. In subsequent months I was often tempted to cut off the rest of the world and just focus on my writing journey. However, I continued to be involved in my outer journey as I recognised the energising effect on me from maintaining this balance.

Through our inner journey we continue to discover new parts of our Self that our present world does not always encourage us to express. As we experience this incongruence we can feel stress, tension and frustration. This is a signal that we need to make changes in our personal world if we are not to experience ongoing frustration, which can finally lead to anger, or perhaps more commonly, depression, illness or addictive behaviour.

To continue creating a personal world congruent with our evolving Self we need to continue exploring our outer world. Through trial and error we find new ways of living through placing ourself in new circumstances and observing how we feel within them. This exploration helps us to find places, people and activities that enable us to express all the newly found parts of our Self.

This outer journey requires the masculine side of our nature. It tests our ability to take control, to take a stance, to use our discriminating intellect, and to be able to analyse and then express our needs. How easily we are able to embrace our outer journey depends on a variety of factors, including our personality, our past experiences, our present lifestyle, and our ability to assert ourself.

When I was a child, young girls were often told 'be careful', 'take care', 'don't wander too far'. If this is said enough, a child will begin to think there is something out there that can harm them. Girls of my generation were also encouraged to conform, be compliant and please others. These directives given when young can still be present as self-limiting inner messages and may stop us taking on the necessary outer journey to create a new personal world.

In her book *The Girl Within*, Emily Hancock, a psychologist, identifies a turning point in a girl's life—the period between ages eight and ten and the onset of adolescence—as the time when a girl crystallises a distinct and vital sense of self, which she then loses in the process of growing up female. Women in Hancock's study reported that at this age they had a sense of independence. One of the participants, Megan, reported, 'At nine, I can remember walking on a fence, all around a park, thinking I would really like to be nine forever. I remember having a real sense of joy and confidence about negotiating the world on my own.' When this description was read out to a group of women all of them could recognise themselves in that nine-year-old girl.

> But melancholy followed on the heels of excitement as the women grew subdued and even tearful as each in turn realised how early she had put this girl aside, replacing her vitality with feminine compliance.

In an effort to conform to feminine values, many girls put aside this exploring, adventurous, vital girl. As adolescent girls in the 1950s and 1960s we often focused our attention and energy on boys and their world. A sense of confidence often came more from having a boyfriend rather than anything to do with our self. We sat passively watching them play their sport and music. Energy was focused on their world and how they might be kept by our side, rather than putting energy into our own pursuits and dreams. We stopped climbing trees, walking on top of fences, taking risks and exploring our world. We stopped creating a personal world of which we were the centre.

At midlife, many of us need to continually reconnect with that vital, adventurous nine-year-old girl if we are to create a personal world congruent with our Self. And, of course, it is not only in our physical world that we need to connect with her.

In my mid-thirties, when I started my business consulting to organisations I often experienced anxiety as I put myself into new situations. For example, I knew that I had to get used to public speaking and this was something I had always found quite nerve-racking. However, I was determined to give it my best shot and so put up with anxiety-ridden, sleepless nights and butterflies in my stomach. I certainly used whatever strategies I could think of to help me—positive visualisation, meditation, positive self-talk—however, in the end I accepted that feeling anxious was an understandable part of taking on a new challenge. And as I became more practised at public speaking my anxiety lessened and my confidence in my ability to impact on my world increased.

Certain things stand out for me about times such as this when I have connected with my adventurous self:

1 I have to take myself *way out of my comfort zone*.
2 I have to be able to do it alone. Others might encourage me, but eventually *I have to find the confidence and belief within myself.*
3 Finally, after I have met the new challenge it is important for me to take time out and acknowledge what I have accomplished. Often I sense a part of myself has come alive, a part of myself that had been buried for many years. This then gives me greater vitality and confidence to challenge many of my other internal self-limiting beliefs.

Take some time now to ask yourself these questions:

• Are you creating a personal world to suit your Self?
• Are there personal challenges you are avoiding?
• Is there something stopping you?

- Do you need to reconnect with your vital, adventurous self?
- If so, what do you need to do to make contact with her?
- How could you maintain your connection with your adventurous self throughout the rest of your life?

I am not suggesting you need to take up public speaking or rock climbing. Start with a small step where you are assured of some success. Do not overwhelm yourself by setting the bar too high. Perhaps you have always wanted to do a course in photography, or art, or astrology. Or you have dreamt of a career in journalism. What is it you would like to do? What's stopping you? Are there genuine reasons why you aren't working towards your dreams or are they convenient excuses so you don't have to move out of your comfort zone?

If you fear going by yourself, take a friend who shares your interest. I would recommend, however, sometimes going alone. For I have found that when I go to courses alone, I draw on inner resources and bring out aspects of myself I otherwise may not do if I had a friend with me. Also, a conversation with a course participant around your shared interest can develop into an ongoing friendship and these conversations are more likely to occur if you don't have a buddy with you.

As we continue our inner and outer journey through life our personal world is likely to change as our perception of self changes. At the same time, our perception of self changes as we have new experiences in a changing personal world. For example, in my late thirties, as I spent time meditating and daydreaming I sensed an inner desire to explore my creative side. I then had to take control and create opportunities to explore the creative world. I spent several years attending workshops on watercolour painting, drumming, dancing, singing and writing.

As I did this, I was exploring the outer creative world and at the same time exploring my inner creative self. By putting myself in a different outer world I hoped to find out something new about my inner world. I learnt that some of these activities connected me to my Self, others didn't. I used my masculine, discriminating powers to determine which activities most fulfilled my yearnings. Some helped me uncover significant parts of my Self. Others didn't. When I did reveal a part of my Self it meant that my personal world changed, sometimes quite significantly. For example, it was through attending some writing classes that I eventually realised my potential and enjoyment for writing. This discovery of my 'writing self' has dramatically changed my personal world this year, and perhaps for the rest of my life.

It is a fine balance between our inner and outer journey, and to keep this balance we need to keep on using both our masculine and feminine energies. When I first started seeking out solitude and focusing more on my inner journey, I was drawn to spending lengths of time in meditative practices. I had spent so many years using my masculine energy to keep my busy life 'on track', I now believe that I was being drawn to my inner world as compensation. I meditated regularly during the day as a way of making contact with my inner self. Since then I have found a variety of ways to continue this inner journey without doing it in such a structured, concentrated and focused way.

For each of us, the amount of time we need for our inner journey and the amount of time and energy we need for our outer journey will vary at different stages in our life. I now know I do benefit from spending time daily on a Self-reflective, centering pursuit, whether it be writing, meditating, or walking in the garden. I also benefit from taking an outer journey out of my comfort zone from time to time. We need to observe ourselves to determine how much time we need for our individual journeys. I no longer believe that to find my Self I need to sit in solitude for hours, or days or weeks on end. Rather, I notice my Self, my inner world rubbing shoulders with my outer world. One complements the other as they both expand. As long as I am vigilant as I am living each day, both benefit as I maintain a balance between my inner and outer journey.

22

Nurturing your self

Be gentle on your self

When I started working as a consultant in my mid-thirties one of my main areas of interest was stress management. It is said that psychologists often are attracted to working in areas they need most themselves. This was certainly the case for me at this time of my life.

In the middle to late 1980s stress was a new 'buzzword'. At first I assumed it was just that—some new fad that would come and go. However, the more I read about it, the more it helped me make sense of what I had been experiencing with my own health. Over the previous years I had often visited the doctor because of poor digestion, sharp swings in energy and mood after eating certain foods, muscle tension and gynaecological problems.

In my reading I learnt that every day we are placed under stress, evoking in us the stress response. Much of the time we manage stress successfully and without much effort. When the stress response is induced, certain physiological reactions occur in our body simultaneously, triggered by the secretion of a hormone in our brain. These reactions are automatic, we have little control of them and often we are unaware that they are happening. This automatic stress response results in:

- increased heart rate;
- increased blood pressure;
- increased breathing rate and shallow breathing;
- decreased blood flow to the digestive system as it is diverted towards the head, lungs, brain and muscles, preparing us for action;
- increased release of sugar into the bloodstream for quick energy;
- increased release of cholesterol into the bloodstream;
- increased oxygen requirements;
- increased sweating;
- increased alertness of the mind; and
- increased muscle tension.

At its extreme, the stress response is known as Hans Selye's now famous 'fight or flight' response. The 'fight or flight' response is an adaptive response within all of us and was useful when we were running away from a sabre-toothed tiger. Unfortunately, today we may also evoke it as we are sitting in a traffic jam; asserting ourself in a difficult situation with an unreasonable teenager, friend or colleague; or as we run around meeting the deadlines of the myriad of tasks of our everyday life. As the higher part of our brain tells us it is inappropriate to flee or fight the traffic jam, the difficult teenager, colleagues and friends or our responsibilities, our body becomes flooded with contradictory messages and reactions. If this response occurs often or over a long period of time, it can eventually lead to fatigue and a variety of physical, emotional and intellectual problems. Examples of these are:

- digestive disorders, blood sugar problems, aggravation of asthma, skin problems, elevated blood pressure and a variety of other health problems;
- irritability resulting in poor interpersonal relationships;
- distractability and low concentration resulting in inability to make effective decisions;
- feeling on edge all the time resulting in difficulty in enjoying leisure and recreation time; and
- repeatedly going over negative thoughts and images, leading to poor self-esteem.

As I ran stress management courses I explained to participants that ultimately we need to find a way to live our life where we are only using this response sparingly. I wasn't suggesting that we eliminate all stress from our life. If this was the case we would be dead! Rather, we need to learn to notice when extreme stress has built up in our body, look at what is causing it, and then decide on appropriate changes. We can decide to make changes around the situation, leave the situation, or change our thinking about the situation. For example, if we notice we are arriving to work in the morning over-stressed from all the traffic we are forced to drive through, we can decide to:

- find another way to drive to work, which although longer has less traffic;
- find work closer to home or set up a home-based business so we don't have to deal with daily traffic; or
- think differently about traffic jams. For example, substitute 'I can't stand this. I hate wasting my time' with 'I would

prefer not to be in traffic. However, I can't do anything about it. I will listen to some music and focus on something constructive or relaxing.'

As I continued to run these courses I started to 'practise what I preached'. I began to observe myself. I gradually started to make many of the changes I have mentioned in this book. I removed much extreme stress from my life by either changing the situation or changing my thinking about it.

I also realised this wasn't the complete story. As well as diminishing the number of times I experienced an extreme build-up of stress in my body, I enhanced my sense of well-being as I found a variety of ways to invoke the relaxation response, the reverse of the stress response. I introduced into my daily life a variety of activities that I now perceive as 'nurturing my self'. The beauty of all these activities is that I have control of them and so I can bring them into my life whenever I choose. I am not relying on others for my nurturing.

As mentioned in previous chapters, women and men are androgynous. Each of us has masculine potential to be strong, individual, assertive, independent, leading; and feminine potential to be trusting, accepting, loving, compassionate, caring, passive and nurturing. If we use too many of the masculine qualities we are too hard on our self. If we use too many of the feminine qualities we are too soft on our self. From midlife on, our task is to balance out these qualities in our self. A bit like the saying, 'Not too hard, not too soft, but just right.'

Our Western culture overvalues the masculine qualities at the expense of the feminine ones. We tend to reward the masculine qualities of strength, independence and focused hard work with admiration, prestige and generous salaries. As a result, in many aspects of life, both women and men are too hard on themselves. At midlife we need to be able to step back from this influence and start identifying more with our feminine energy.

Traditionally, a woman learnt from a young age to develop her feminine qualities in relation to others. She has an inclination to show trust, acceptance, love, compassion, care and nurturing in her relationships. Unfortunately rarely has she been encouraged to show these qualities towards herself. Do you? Now when my friends or I are feeling low we say to each other, 'Be gentle on your self', for we all know given our life training we all tend to be 'hard on our self'.

When I ask clients how they nurture themselves they often don't know what I mean. Even when I explain that I am asking what they do to take care of themselves they still can't answer because they haven't thought about it before. Often there isn't anything they do for themselves. I suggest they gradually build up a program of showing ways to be 'gentle on themself'.

How do you nurture your self? I'll explain to you some of the things I have introduced to my life during midlife transition. As you read, I suggest you make a list of what you are doing at the moment to nurture your self.

For balance and a sense of wellbeing we need to nurture our self physically, emotionally, intellectually and spiritually. Some activities nurture us on many different levels. I attend yoga classes at a local women's gym three times a week. I find yoga nurtures me on all four levels. My body physically relaxes as I stretch. At times I quietly sob on my mat, releasing emotions that have built up during my day. As my mind relaxes I spontaneously have insights about my life. By the end of the hour session I feel more centered on my self.

I nurture myself by eating the right food. If we do not put the right petrol in our car it eventually does not run as well. In fact, one day it might stop completely. It is the same with our body. If we look after our body by giving it what it needs to remain physically healthy, it will reward us by allowing us to move through life with energy and vitality. I therefore notice myself and my diet—not for body shape, but rather for energy levels and a sense of wellbeing.

I have read that our city-bought foods are often low in vitamins and minerals, either because of the way they are grown, or because of the time lapse between when they were picked and when we eat them. I have also read of the effect on my immune system of the toxins in my environment. I therefore buy fresh, organic food when possible. I also supplement my diet with minerals and vitamins. I took professional advice before doing this.

Many years ago I went through a phase of being very strict on myself and my family around what we ate. By the end of the year I decided that although we were physically well, I was creating psychological problems around eating in the family. I was learning the need for balance—not too hard and not too soft.

I nurture my self by watching carefully what I feed my mind. As much as possible I fill my mind with healthy thoughts and ideas. I watch little television. I rarely watch the news, but rather keep informed by reading weekend newspapers, talking with friends and listening to the radio. I find wonderful programs on morning and evening radio that are informative, entertaining and uplifting. I have always found carefully chosen books to be good brain food. During the more turbulent times of midlife transition I found great solace in several books. I used them regularly to help uplift my thoughts. They tended to be books with short passages or quotations that I could easily dip into before going to sleep or perhaps before going out. In fact, any time of the day. I have subsequently recommended them to friends and clients and they also have found them beneficial. Two books of quotations I used often during the most turbulent times of midlife transition are *Illuminations: Visions for Change and Self Acceptance* and *Inneractions: Visions to Bring Your Inner and Outer World into Harmony*, both by Stephen Paul and Gary Max Collins. I also suggest to clients to browse in bookshops as they can be led to a book that is just right for them.

During midlife I have introduced a variety of enjoyable exercise into my life. When young I tended to exercise by playing sport. Now I walk, swim and cycle. I have been told that walking is the best exercise to maintain my bone density and so I tend to walk for at least half an hour daily. In recent years I have greatly enjoyed walking with a neighbour, Penny. She is also a psychologist and as we walk and talk we are nurturing ourselves physically, emotionally, intellectually and spiritually. When walking alone I take my discman as I find walking to music with a strong beat helps me to stride out. Compared to my sport-orientated earlier life, I now try to choose a balanced approach to exercise with a focus on enjoyment and wellbeing as well as exercise.

To nurture myself I have placed around me people who encourage me to pursue my dreams and to keep creating a life that feels right for me. Many of my relationships have changed at midlife. I choose to spend my leisure time around people with whom I can easily share my feelings and thoughts and be completely myself. I listen to them talk about their world, as they listen to me talk about mine. My relationships with my young adult children have dramatically changed. We relax and

Tips from Bertie to nurture your self

- Take rests often.
- Run to greet those you love.
- On first waking, stretch your limbs.
- Take time out to daydream.
- Be conscious of who you allow into your personal space.
- Find ways to experience the ecstasy of fresh air and wind on your face.
- When you are feeling joyful, dance around and wag your tail.
- Delight in simple pleasures such as a walk in the garden or a lie in the sun.
- Keep searching and digging until you find those precious things you have buried.
- Make your needs known—a gentle reminder is often enough.
- Nuzzle up often to those you love.
- When it feels cold outside, curl up where it is warm—and dream.

share with each other our thoughts and feelings about our lives. I believe this is healthy for all of us.

As well as the above, I also nurture myself by:

- burning aromatherapy oils and incense;
- listening to all kinds of music depending on my mood;
- enjoying a full body or reflexology massage;
- taking a bath with essential oils;

- watching the moon from my front verandah;
- making time for all the things I love to do such as dance, sing, drum and chat with friends; and
- structuring my days so that as much as possible there is an easy flow to them.

How are you nurturing your self?

23

A vision for your future

*Our deepest fear is not that we are inadequate. Our deepest fear is
that we are powerful beyond measure. It is our light, not our darkness,
that most frightens us. We ask ourselves, who am I to be brilliant,
gorgeous, talented, fabulous? Actually, who are you not to be? . . .
And as we let our own light shine, we unconsciously give other people
permission to do the same. As we're liberated from our own fear, our
presence automatically liberates others.*

Marianne Williamson, *A Return to Love*

This morning I picked up my journal and read an entry in it
for the first time since writing it this time last year. I was
surprised to read:

And now at the end of this millennium my big goal is to write
about where I have come from and where I want to go.

I had no idea I was thinking that way a year ago. Oh! The value
of keeping a journal.

When I started writing *Navigating Midlife* I did not realise that
so much of my focus would be on my own story and 'where I
have come from'. After reading this journal entry I can now see
that for months, if not years before I started writing, there was

a force within me suggesting that this was something I needed to do.

As I write this last chapter I do sense that I am now ready to look at 'where I want to go'. From my reading and observations I believe I am moving on to the next developmental stage, middle adulthood, a movement that usually happens for women between the ages of 45 to 50. As with other stages in my life, I don't believe there will be a tidy finishing off of my midlife transition before I move on to this next stage. Rather, I am now moving on while still dealing with some of the developmental tasks from the earlier stage. I continue to gather in projections and question some of my attitudes. For example, I still too easily get caught up in 'doing' and still need to put energy into noticing this in myself and then pulling back to a more balanced combination of being and doing. It could take years before the effect of the thorough training I had in the first half of my life wears off enough for me to find my own true balance. I will continue to do midlife developmental tasks for several years to come as I move into this next stage, middle adulthood.

Not all women will be ready to move on to middle adulthood by their late forties. Luckily, right through life we can go back at any stage and complete a developmental task that was for one reason or another not completed earlier. Some women reach 50 still not accepting their individuality or their aloneness. These women need to spend much time and energy doing the work preferably completed in the teens and early twenties. They need to push themselves to do things on their own, exploring their individuality. This is the only way they will develop the inner and outer resources for creating a fulfilling personal world for their second half of life. This can particularly be necessary for women who went from the family home to marriage and reached midlife never having spent time on their own. Many women eventually manage to create this alone time. One woman I know lived away from her husband and three grown-up children for a year. She explained to her husband and children that she wasn't leaving them permanently, she just wanted some time on her own. She visited them regularly. After a year she happily went back to live with her husband and one of her children—her two other children having decided it was time to leave. However, it was a different woman who moved back home. While away she had created a life of her own, which she continued to enjoy alongside the life with her husband and family. Other women take long periods of time away by themselves, often as a holiday or a work commitment.

Some women resist the tasks of midlife transition and decide to continue their life very much as it has been in the first half of life. They continue to perform roles and live their life mostly in a relational capacity as perhaps wife, mother, daughter, sister, friend or carer. They wonder why their life lacks a feeling of inner excitement and meaning. As if something is missing but they can't quite work out what or why.

However, between the ages of 45 and 50, many women complete most of the tasks necessary for midlife transition. Due to much hard work and soul-searching during midlife we are rewarded by having a clearer idea of who we are. We are also beginning to create the personal world we wish to place around our Self as we move into the second half of life. As we have gathered in many of our projections we feel more complete in our Self. Some of our relationships from the first half of life have gone. Others have changed. And many of our relationships are deeper and more authentic.

We no longer look to others for advice on how we should be. Occasionally we might catch ourselves wondering what others think of us, however we notice the tendency in ourselves, and remember that no longer do we want to seek out another's approval for how we should live. We only want to look to our Self and our inner core of values. This does not mean that we are selfish, for as we connect with our Self and our values we connect with the basic human attitudes of compassion, tolerance and acceptance. As we accept more of our Self, including those parts of our Self we did not want to own in the first half of life, we use these attitudes in relation to our Self. And as we do this, we use these attitudes in relation to others.

There will still be times of turbulence and strong emotions ahead as we continue to make changes and create our future. As we sell the family home, or leave behind the career of many years, such decisions—even though well thought through and looked forward to—are accompanied by strong feelings as we let go another part of our 'old life'. Other times we feel bewildered by incongruent feelings of knowing we are getting older, yet feeling younger, more alive and freer than we have for a long time. We sense a shedding of responsibilities and at the same time enjoy the freedom to commit time and energy to the life we wish to create for our Self from here on.

Much of the literature talks about middle adulthood as a time when individuals increasingly desire to withdraw from public life. Much of the writing and research has been done on and by men. Comments made about women have been more as an added extra. Women's and men's journeys are often very different. In the first half of life men have traditionally spent many years where their primary focus has been in the public arena, developing a career and 'a place in the world'. By the end of midlife transition these same men want to focus more on their relationships as these have been put on the back-burner while they forged ahead in the world.

A few women of the baby boomer generation have followed this male pattern and as they reach their fifties are also looking for more connection through relationships in their lives. However, many women, including those who have had an ongoing professional life, have had as a necessary primary focus in the first half of life the tasks around maintaining a family and a home. I believe these women can get to the end of midlife transition and have a different need to men. They sense that their family responsibilities are decreasing, and as well as looking forward to increasing time for themselves, they relish the idea of having time to make a significant, personally mean-ingful contribution to the bigger, outer world.

So as I leave midlife behind and move into the next stage I am thinking: *'Given what I now understand to be my Self and my core values, what type of life do I want to create for my second half of life?'* If I imagine my life evolving during the next five years what might it look like if I commit myself to my core values? I don't necessarily mean a snapshot image, for this may be too constricting. Rather, a general impression of how I will shape my life to express my core values.

I still have children living with me and so some changes I plan for the next stage of my life I will put on hold. Others I have already started putting into place. As I think of what is important to me, what values will guide me, I find it useful to use the stem, 'I will . . .' Where there are aspects of my present life that I wish to continue, I use the stem, 'I will continue to . . .' The following list is of things that I have decided are important for me; you might like to make a list of your own. Try and list at least three things you are ready to commit to. For the moment, I suggest you not be too specific. For example, write, 'I will live somewhere near the coast', rather than, 'I will live near Byron Bay'.

MY LIST

- I will continue to use my inner feminine intuition and feeling to remain in touch with my Self and my inner guide. I will also use my inner feminine side to remain relaxed, self-nurturing, giving and flexible about how I lead my life.
- I will continue to use my masculine energy to be disciplined, focused, assertive and courageous to ensure I continue creating a personal world of work and leisure time that is meaningful, challenging and enjoyable.
- One day soon I will live simply. Increasingly I notice how much of my energy goes into maintaining a large home. For the moment I feel thankful that I have so much space as I enjoy sharing my home life with my children and my niece. However, in the future I will live differently. My home will be small, less cluttered, and as with my present home, in a situation where I can easily enjoy nature.

And I will continue to:

- create time for solitude;
- have a lifestyle where I have daily contact with the physical, natural world. Increasingly I cherish walking in nature, whether at the beach, in the mountains or in a garden. Preferably, on a daily basis I will with ease be able to feel the wind in my hair and watch the birds;
- live a lifestyle where I can regularly do exercise such as walk, swim and do yoga;

- eat healthy meals and preferably, eventually grow much of my own food;
- make time to relax through music, dance, creative pursuits, family and friends;
- create a life where I can maintain regular contact with my children and close friends; and
- put my time and energy into work projects that have meaning for me and at the same time use my knowledge and talents. I will work in a way that my chosen lifestyle is not compromised, except for self-determined periods of time.

Have you made a list? You may want to spend quite a while thinking it through. I suggest that once you have completed it, you put it in your bedside drawer or in another personal place, in an enclosed envelope and make a mark in your diary to look at it in six months' time. You may be surprised with the progress you have made in moving your life in a direction that reflects your core values.

As I now read the story of my first half of life, so much of it seems like a preparation for my second half of life. And my story will continue, as will yours, as we take into this second half of life a new sense of Self and life purpose. When I look back to myself and my life in my mid-thirties I appreciate that I am also taking into this second half of life a 'me' that is more real, self-directed, living in process and tolerant and accepting of others. I now enjoy deeper relationships, travel both an inner and outer journey with more ease, and enjoy creativity and all it brings to my life.

So as we complete navigating midlife, we cross the threshold into the second half of life. We continue to create this new life, guided by our core values which flow from our sense of Self and an intuitive understanding of the real meaning and purpose of our life. And as we sense this increasing confidence, we have a feeling that our own life is just beginning.

THE JOURNEY NEVER ENDS

Bibliography

Barger, N. & Kirby, L. 1995, *The Challenge of Change in Organisations*, Davies-Black Publishing, Palo Alto, California

Benson, Dr H. 1975, *The Relaxation Response*, William Morrow and Company, New York

Bolen, J. S. 1984, *Goddesses in Every Woman*, Harper-Collins, San Francisco

Brennan, A. & Brewi, J. 1991, *Mid-Life: Psychological and Spiritual Perspectives*, The Crossroad Publishing Co., New York

—— 1999, *Midlife Spirituality and Jungian Archetypes*, Nicholas-Hays, York Beach

Bridges, W. 1991, *Managing Transitions*, Addison-Wesley, Reading, Mass

Cameron, J. 1995, *The Artist's Way: A Spiritual Path to Higher Creativity*, Pan Books, London

Corlett, E. & Millner, N. 1993, *Navigating Midlife*, Consulting Psychologists Press, Palo Alto, California

Dante, A. 1974, *The Divine Comedy: Hell*, translated by Dorothy L. Sayers, Penguin Books

Dessaix, R. 1998, *And So Forth*, Pan Macmillan, Sydney

Druckman, D. & Bjork, A. 1991, *In the Mind's Eye: Enhancing Human Performance*, National Academy Press, Washington, DC

Fincher, S. 1991, *Creating Mandalas for Insight, Healing and Self-Expression*, Shambhala, New York

Gawain, S. 1989, *Return to the Garden*, Nataraj Publishing, California

Hancock, E. 1989, *The Girl Within*, Ballantyne Books, Random House, Toronto

Hay, L. 1987, *You Can Heal Your Life*, Hay House Inc., California

Hillman, J. 1990, *The Essential James Hillman: A Blue Fire*, Thomas Moore (ed.), Routledge

Hollis, J. 1993, *The Middle Passage: From Misery To Meaning In Midlife*, Inner City Books, Toronto

Hopcke, R. 1997, *There Are No Accidents*, Riverhead Books, New York

Johnson, R. 1986, *Inner Work; Using Dreams and Active Imagination for Personal Growth*, HarperSanFrancisco, San Francisco

—— 1989, *She: Understanding Feminine Psychology*, HarperSanFrancisco, San Francisco

—— 1990, *Femininity Lost and Regained*, Harper Perennial, HarperCollins Publishers, New York

—— 1991, *Owning Your Own Shadow*, HarperSanFrancisco, San Francisco

Jones, C. 1989, *The Search for Meaning Collection*, ABC Enterprises, Sydney

Jung, Carl G. 1933, *Modern Man In Search Of A Soul*, Harcourt-Brace, New York

——1956, *Two Essays on Analytical Psychology*, 2nd edn., translated by R. F. C. Hull, Meridian Books, New York

—— 1971, *Psychological Types*, Princeton University Press, Princeton, NJ

—— 1973, *Mandala Symbolism*, Princeton University Press, Princeton, NJ

—— 1982, *Aspects of the Feminine*, translated by R. F. C. Hull, Bollingen Series XX, Princeton University Press

—— 1983, *Memories, Dreams and Reflections*, Aniela Jaffe (ed.), translated by Richard and Clara Winston, Vintage Books, New York

—— 1990, *Man And His Symbols*, Penguin, London

Levinson, D. 1996, *The Seasons of a Woman's Life*, Alfred A. Knopf, New York

Lindbergh, A. M. 1983, *Gift From the Sea*, Random House, New York

Lowen, Dr A. 1980, *Fear Of Life*, Collier Macmillan Publishers, London

Mackenzie, V. 1998, *Cave In The Snow*, Bloomsbury, London

Macquarie Concise Dictionary, 3rd edn. 1998, The Macquarie Library Pty Ltd, Sydney

Myers, I. 1998, *Introduction to Type*, 6th edn, Katherine D. Myers and Linda K. Kirby (eds), Consulting Psychologists Press, Palo Alto, California

Myers, I. with Myers, P. 1990, *Gifts Differing*, Consulting Psychologists Press, Palo Alto, California

Nietzsche, F. 1972, *The Portable Nietzsche*, translated by Walter Kaufmann, Viking, New York

O'Connor, Dr P. 1981, *Understanding the Mid-Life Crisis*, Sun Books Pty Ltd, Australia

—— 1988, *Understanding Jung*, Reed Books Australia

Paul, S. & Collins, G. 1990, *Illuminations: Visions For Change and Self Acceptance*, HarperCollins Publishers, New York

—— 1992, *Inneractions: Visions To Bring Your Inner and Outer World into Harmony*, HarperCollins Publishers, New York

Progoff, Dr I. 1973, *Jung, Synchronicity and Human Destiny: Noncausal Dimensions of Human Experience*, Dell Publishing Co., New York

—— 1981, *Jung's Psychology and its Social Meaning*, Dialogue House, New York

—— 1992, *At a Journal Workshop*, Dialogue House, New York

Quenk, A. & Quenk, N. 1995, *Dream Thinking*, Davies-Black, A Division of Consulting Psychologist Press Inc., Palo Alto, California

Quenk, N. 1993, *Beside Ourselves: Our Hidden Personality in Everyday Life*, CPP Books, A Division of Consulting Psychologist Press Inc., Palo Alto, California

Russell, W. 1998, *Shirley Valentine*, Metheun, London

Samuels, A. 1985, *Jung and the Post-Jungians*, Routledge, New York

Sark 1994, *Living Juicy*, Celestial Arts Berkeley, California

Sheehy, G. 1976, *Passages: Predictable Crises of Adult Life*, Dutton, New York

—— 1981, *Pathfinders: Overcoming the Crisis of Adult Life and Finding Your Own Path to Well-Being*, William Morrow, New York

Spencer, A. 1982, *Seasons: Women's Search For Self Through Life's Stages*, Paulist Press, New Jersey

Stein, M. 1983, *In Midlife: A Jungian Perspective*, Spring Publications, Dallas

St James, E. 1996, *Living The Simple Life: A Guide To Scaling Down and Enjoying More*, Hyperion, New York

Stone, Dr H. & Winkelman, Dr S. 1989, *Embracing Our Selves*, New World Library, California

Storr, A. 1993, *Jung: Selected Writings*, Fontana Paperbacks, London

Viorst, J. 1986, *Necessary Losses*, Simon & Schuster, Australia

Von Franz, M. 1975, *Carl Gustav Jung: His Myth In Our Time*, Little, Brown & Co.

Wehr, S. 1989, *Jung and Feminism: Liberating Archetypes*, Beacon Press, Boston

Whitmont, E. 1969, *The Symbolic Quest: Basic Concepts of Analytical Psychology*, Princeton University Press, Princeton

Williamson, M. 1992, *A Return to Love: Reflections on the Principles of a Course in Miracles*, HarperCollins, New York

Woodman, M. 1989, *Addiction to Perfection: The Still Unravished Bride*, Inner City Books, Canada

—— 1993, *Conscious Femininity: Interviews with Marion Woodman*, Inner City Books, Canada

Index

For information on Robyn Vickers-Willis's
courses and seminars, visit her website at
www.navigatingmidlife.com